# Building Spelling Skills

## Book 6

Written and designed by Garry J. Moes
Editors: Michael J. McHugh
Dr. Paul D. Lindstrom

A PUBLICATION OF
*Christian Liberty Press*

# TABLE OF CONTENTS

# PREFACE

Dear Teacher or Parent:

In this Book 6 of the *Building Spelling Skills* series, students are led through an examination of the great diversity and variation in spellings of the rich sounds of the English language. This is shown through studies of vowels, consonants, consonant combinations, prefixes, suffixes, synonyms, homonyms, antonyms, irregularities and exceptions. Students are again given numerous opportunities to write and rewrite the words in each Unit Word List. Extensive practice, in the form of repetitive writing of the selected words, is a major tool in learning to spell English words.

This book also seeks to build vocabulary. To this end, the student is given opportunity to use some spelling words in the context of sentences. Because many of the words in each unit are more advanced in difficulty, students are encouraged to make extensive use of the dictionary and thesaurus to understand precise meanings and usages. The final lesson in each unit is designed to highlight internal word components and the arrangement of key spelling features of the unit's list words.

Various word games and puzzles are included in most units. These are intended to guide the student into carefully recognizing the arrangement of letters and/or syllables in selected list words, an exercise which is important in light of the many irregularities in spelling the words of the English language.

Instructors are encouraged to keep reading and spelling in close fellowship with each other during the teaching process. It is also helpful to keep in mind that there are no shortcuts on the road to developing good spellers. Good spellers are developed by a teacher's hard work, persistence and encouragement, not to mention the same for the student.

## TEACHING SUGGESTIONS

In addition to the instructions given for each unit and lesson, the following approaches are offered by way of suggestion to help teachers better guide their students to good spelling:

1. Read all of the words from the Unit Word List aloud with your student.

2. Emphasize to the student the primary phonetic keys to the words in the lesson.

3. Quiz the student by asking him to write each of the words from the lesson on separate paper as you read each of them aloud.

4. Check the accuracy of the student's written work and help the student understand why he misspelled certain words.

5. Have your student provide the correct spelling for any words he misspelled on separate paper or on a chalkboard.

6. Show the student how some of the words from the unit are used in a sentence. This exercise will help to improve the student's comprehension, pronunciation skills, and vocabulary. Students should be encouraged to use some of their spelling words in sentences of their own choosing.

7. Conclude each unit with a review of that unit's words and a final test. Finally, you may wish to review words from the current unit or previous ones before starting into a new unit or exercise.

# ALPHABET

Aa Bb Cc Dd Ee Ff Gg Hh Ii Jj Kk Ll Mm

Nn Oo Pp Qq Rr Ss Tt Uu Vv Ww Xx Yy Zz

## CURSIVE ALPHABET

*Aa Bb Cc Dd Ee*
*Ff Gg Hh Ii Jj*
*Kk Ll Mm Nn*
*Oo Pp Qq Rr Ss*
*Tt Uu Vv Ww*
*Xx Yy Zz*

# *LEARNING*

# *HOW TO*

# *SPELL WORDS*

1. Look at the word. Study every letter.

2. Say the word to yourself.

3. Say it again aloud, and then spell it.

4. Copy the word on paper, naming the letters as you write.

5. Close your spelling book, and test yourself.
   Write the word.
   Do not worry if you do not get it right the first time.

6. Open your spelling book again. Check the word.

7. Study the word one more time, and test yourself
   by writing the word again.

\* \* \* \* \*

*As with all of your school work, always remember to ask God to help you learn and understand what you are doing.  Thank Him for His help with every lesson.*

# U*NIT 1*

# SPELLING LONG 'A'

| | |
|---|---|
| brace | portray |
| glaze | crayfish |
| crazy | playmate |
| plague | skein |
| quaint | freight |
| frail | they |
| maim | whey |
| strain | break |
| chaise | greatness |
| bray | gauge |

## *LESSON 1*

Study these list words, using the
study plan on page 7.

## *LESSON 2*  VOCABULARY / DICTIONARY

Use these list words in sentences. Consult a dictionary, if necessary, to understand their meanings. You may
use any tense (past, present, or future) of verbs, either singular or plural form of nouns, and comparative (-er)
or superlative (-est) forms of adjectives and adverbs, if you are careful to spell these alternative forms correctly.

**chaise** _____

_____

**quaint** _____

_____

**skein** _____

_____

**glaze** _____

_____

**plague** _____

_____

**whey** _____

_____

**crayfish** _____

_____

# LESSON 3

Write each of your list words three times on a separate sheet of paper.

## FINER THINGS

Complete these sentences with list words.

1. The old woman seems quite _____ after her long illness.

2. Skydiving seemed like a _____ idea to Jenna until she actually tried it.

3. Mom coated the roast duck with a _____ of orange sauce.

4. My little brother was lonesome when his _____ had to stay indoors due to illness last week.

5. Grandma needed another _____ of yarn to finish her knitting.

6. The old couple relaxed on _____ lounges (chairs) on the ship's deck as a tropical breeze caressed the vessel.

7. Pharoah allowed the Israelites to leave Egypt after the tenth _____ brought death to the firstborn of the Egyptians.

8. Alex will _____ Abraham Lincoln in the Presidents' Day pageant.

9. Brittany thought curds and _____ might be an acceptable lunch for Little Miss Muffit, but she would prefer macaroni and cheese.

10. The purpose of a righteous war is not simply to kill and _____ the enemy, but to bring about justice and peace.

11. On our vacation in Maine, we visited a _____ village with ornate houses and picturesque shops.

12. The car's gasoline _____ indicated it was time to refuel.

# LESSON 4

Take your first practice test on all words in your Unit 1 word list. Write the words on a separate sheet of paper as they are read to you. Write any words you misspelled on your practice test five times on another sheet.

## WHAT'S IN A WORD?

The long 'a' sound may be spelled at least seven different ways.
Write list words with each of these spellings.
Earn bonus points by writing non-list words in the unused blanks.

| a | ai | ay | ei |
|---|----|----|----|
| _____ | _____ | _____ | _____ |
| _____ | _____ | _____ | _____ |
| _____ | _____ | _____ | _____ |
| _____ | _____ | _____ | _____ |
| _____ | _____ | _____ | _____ |

| ey | ea | au |
|----|----|----|

**RESEARCH**
**Answer these questions on paper:**

1. Which spellings of long 'a' follow the long-vowel phonics rule?
2. Which are vowel digraphs?
3. What is the long-vowel rule? What is a vowel digraph?

| ey | ea | au |
|----|----|----|
| _____ | _____ | _____ |
| _____ | _____ | _____ |
| _____ | _____ | _____ |
| _____ | _____ | _____ |

# LESSON 5

Take your final test. Write your words in the spaces provided at the back of this book. Start your test with prayer.

10

# U NIT 2

## SPELLING 'A' SOUNDS

### LESSON 1

Study these list words, using the
study plan on page 7.

| | |
|---|---|
| flaunt | thought |
| taunt | wrought |
| heart | gorge |
| hearth | thorn |
| guard | broad |
| drawl | flare |
| squaw | flair |
| sprawl | tear |
| daub | heir |
| fraud | ere |

### LESSON 2   VOCABULARY / DICTIONARY

Use these list words in sentences. Consult a dictionary, if necessary, to understand their meanings. You may
use any tense (past, present, or future) of verbs, either singular or plural form of nouns, and comparative (-er)
or superlative (-est) forms of adjectives and adverbs, if you are careful to spell these alternative forms correctly.

**drawl** _____

_____

**flaunt** _____

_____

**hearth** _____

_____

**daub** _____

_____

**gorge** _____

_____

**flare** _____

_____

**wrought** _____

_____

# LESSON 3

Write each of your list words three times on a separate sheet of paper.

**FINER THINGS**

Complete these Bible verses with list words.

1. "And the peace of God ... will _____ your hearts and your minds in Christ Jesus" (Philippians 4:7, NIV).

2. "...(T)here was given me a _____ in the flesh ... lest I should be exalted above measure" (2 Corinthians 12:7).

3. "...(A)nd _____ is the way, that leadeth to destruction" (Matthew 7:13).

4. "Lord, thou wilt ordain peace for us: for thou also hast _____ all our works in us" (Isaiah 26:12).

5. God "hath in these last days spoken unto us by his Son, whom he hath appointed _____ of all things ..." (Hebrews 1:2).

6. "(A)nd bringing into captivity every _____ to the obedience of Christ" (2 Corinthians 10:5).

7. "(A) broken and a contrite _____ , O God, thou wilt not despise" (Psalm 51:17).

8. "And the Lord said ... how long will it be _____ they believe me, for all the signs which I have shown among them?" (Numbers 14:11).

9. "Now consider this, ye that forget God, lest I _____ you to pieces, and there be none to deliver" (Psalm 50:22).

10. "So it shall be a reproach and a _____ ... when I shall execute judgment in thee in anger" (Ezekiel 5:15).

# LESSON 4

Take your first practice test on all words in your Unit 2 word list. Write the words on a separate sheet of paper as they are read to you. Write any words you misspelled on your practice test five times on another sheet.

## WHAT'S IN A WORD?

ä = au, ea, ua
a̤ = aw, au, ou, o, oa
â = ai, ea, ei, e, a

The various sounds of 'a' may be spelled in the ways shown a the left. Write list words with the spellings of 'a' shown below.

| ai | ëä | au | aw |
|---|---|---|---|

**SYNONYMS**

A word that has the same meaning as another word is a synonym. Write a synonym for:

**ere**

_____

| ou | o |
|---|---|

**HOMONYMS**

Words with different spellings that are pronounced alike are called homonyms. Write two sets of homonyms from your word list.

_____
_____

_____
_____

| oa | ua | eâ |
|---|---|---|

| ei | e | a |
|---|---|---|

# LESSON 5

**TESTING...**
**TESTING...**

Take your final test. Write your words in the spaces provided at the back of this book. Start your test with prayer.

# U NIT 3

# SPELLING 'E' SOUNDS

| | |
|---|---|
| people | deathbed |
| breathe | breath |
| deceased | against |
| steer | leopard |
| sneeze | many |
| fierce | heifer |
| seizure | guess |
| valise | friend |
| key | says |
| quay | bury |

## LESSON 1

Study these list words, using the study plan on page 7.

## LESSON 2    VOCABULARY / DICTIONARY

Use these list words in sentences. Consult a dictionary, if necessary, to understand their meanings. You may use any tense (past, present, or future) of verbs, either singular or plural form of nouns, and comparative (-er) or superlative (-est) forms of adjectives and adverbs, if you are careful to spell these alternative forms correctly.

**key** _____

_____

**quay** _____

_____

**heifer** _____

_____

**valise** _____

_____

**fierce** _____

_____

**seizure** _____

_____

**leopard** _____

_____

# LESSON 3

## FOUNDATIONS

Write each of your list words three times on a separate sheet of paper.

## FINER THINGS

**1** The following paragraph contains ten words that are list words or forms of list words. Circle these words and write them in the blanks.

**After suffering a fierce seizure, the devout old man breathed his last breath as family members stood by his deathbed. A friend of many people, the deceased was buried with much mourning, yet with the knowledge he was with the Lord.**

_____

_____   _____   _____

_____   _____   _____

**2** Write three list words that have different spellings of short 'e' in each of their two syllables. See the chart in Lesson 4 for the various spellings of short 'e.'

_____   _____   _____

**3** Write two list words that are homonyms.

_____   _____

**4** Homographs are two or more words that have the same spelling but are different in meaning and origin, and perhaps in pronunciation. Examples are: "air" (atmosphere) and "air" (a melody); "row" (a straight line), "row" (a noisy quarrel), and "row" (to propel a boat with oars). The list word "steer" is a homograph. In the spaces at the left, write the word "steer" twice and give two definitions for the word. You may consult a dictionary, if necessary.

## LESSON 4

Take your first practice test on all words in your Unit 3 word list. Write the words on a separate sheet of paper as they are read to you. Write any words you misspelled on your practice test five times on another sheet.

## WHAT'S IN A WORD?

Long e = eo, ea, ee, ie, ei, i, ey, uay, y
Short e = ea, e, ai, eo, a, ei, ue, ie, ay, u

Write list words that have these 'e' spellings.

> Notice that the word 'many' has both a short 'e' sound and long 'e' sound. How is each sound spelled? Short e_____ Long e_____

### LONG E

- eo _____
- ea _____
  _____
- ee _____
  _____
- ie _____
- i _____
- ey _____
- uay _____
- ei _____

### SHORT E

- eo _____ a
- ea _____ e
  _____
- ai _____
- ie _____
- a _____
- ei _____ e
- ay _____
- u _____
- ue _____

NOTE: In some dictionaries, the words 'steer' and 'fierce' are not shown to have a long 'e' sound. In these dictionaries, the pronunciation is given as 'i( ə)' or 'î,' which have the sound of something between a short 'i' and long 'e.' Some phonics experts say, however, that 'steer' and 'fierce' have the sound of long 'e.'

## LESSON 5

Take your final test. Write your words in the spaces provided at the back of this book. Ask God to help you with your test.

16

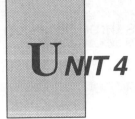

# UNIT 4

## SPELLING 'I' SOUNDS

| | |
|---|---|
| flight | prince |
| writhe | lynx |
| lyre | myth |
| eye | builder |
| magpie | guilt |
| guide | been |
| height | pretty |
| rye | women |
| aisle | busy |
| buy | sieve |

### LESSON 1

Study these list words, using the study plan on page 7.

### LESSON 2   VOCABULARY / DICTIONARY

Use these list words in sentences. Consult a dictionary, if necessary, to understand their meanings. You may use any tense (past, present, or future) of verbs, either singular or plural form of nouns, and comparative (-er) or superlative (-est) forms of adjectives and adverbs, if you are careful to spell these alternative forms correctly.

**writhe** _____

_____

**lyre** _____

_____

**aisle** _____

_____

**lynx** _____

_____

**sieve** _____

_____

**magpie** _____

_____

**guilt** _____

_____

# LESSON 3

## FOUNDATIONS

Write each of your list words three times on a separate sheet of paper.

## FINER THINGS

**1** Write list words that are antonyms for these words.

ugly _____

men _____

idle _____        innocence _____

depth _____        truth _____

princess _____ sell _____

**2** Write the list words you find in the titles of these musical compositions.

*Flight of the Bumblebee* _____

*Comin' Through the Rye* _____

*The Thieving Magpie* _____

*My Pretty Valentine* _____

*Guide Me, O Thou Great Jehovah* _____

*Mansion Builder* _____

*I Have Been Redeemed* _____

# LESSON 4

Take your first practice test on all words in your Unit 4 word list. Write the words on a separate sheet of paper as they are read to you. Write any words you misspelled on your practice test five times on another sheet.

## WHAT'S IN A WORD?

Long i = i, y, ie, ui, ei, ye, uy, ai, eye
Short i = i, y, ui, ee, e, u, ie, o

Write list words that have these 'i' spellings.

| LONG I | SHORT I |
|--------|---------|
| y | i |
| i | y |
| ie | ee |
| ui | e |
| ei | u |
| ye     eye | ie |
| uy | o |
| ai | ui |

# LESSON 5

Take your final test. Write your words in the spaces provided at the back of this book. Ask God to help you with your test.

19

# U<small>NIT</small> 5

| | |
|---|---|
| brogue | prompt |
| shoal | jonquil |
| beau | rocketry |
| courtly | prophecy |
| gourd | prophesy |
| woefully | moccasin |
| doorkeeper | modernism |
| sewn | swamp |
| sown | swashbuckler |
| yeoman | knowledge |

# SPELLING 'O' SOUNDS

## *LESSON 1*

Study these list words, using the
study plan on page 7.

## *LESSON 2*  VOCABULARY/DICTIONARY

Use these list words in sentences. Consult a dictionary, if necessary, to understand their meanings. You may use any tense (past, present, or future) of verbs, either singular or plural form of nouns, and comparative (-er) or superlative (-est) forms of adjectives and adverbs, if you are careful to spell these alternative forms correctly.

**brogue** _____

_____

**shoal** _____

_____

**courtly** _____

_____

**sewn** _____

_____

**prophesy** _____

_____

**modernism** _____

_____

**yeoman** _____

_____

# LESSON 3

Write each of your list words three times on a separate sheet of paper.

**FINER THINGS**

**1** Write two list words that are homonyms.

_____

_____

**2** Write homonyms for these words. Use two list words.

gored _____

bow _____

**3** Write definitions for the six words in the shaded boxes in exercises 1 and 2.

1. _____

2. _____

3. _____

4. _____

5. _____

6. _____

**4** Use list words to complete these sentences.

1. The soldiers' training was _____ inadequate.

2. The students were urged to be _____ in arriving for class to avoid penalties for tardiness.

3. Red-wing blackbirds are some of the most beautiful inhabitants of the _____.

4. Of all the wildflowers growing in the woods, Ashley thought the _____ was most beautiful.

5. The Grand Hotel provided new uniforms for its bellboys and _____ .

6. During World War II, many German scientists became experts in _____ , and some were later employed in the U.S. space program.

7. Allen enjoyed reading _____ stories about pirates, sword-fighting, and adventures on the high seas.

8. Adam and Eve were commanded not to eat of the tree of the _____ of good and evil (Genesis 2:17).

# LESSON 4

Take your first practice test on all words in your Unit 5 word list. Write the words on a separate sheet of paper as they are read to you. Write any words you misspelled on your practice test five times on another sheet.

## WHAT'S IN A WORD?

Spellings for the long o sound = o, oa, ow, ou, oe, eau, eo, ew
Spellings for short o and other o sounds = o, ou, oo, a, ow
Write list words having these spellings of the 'o' sound.

**o** _____

_____

_____

**a** _____

_____

_____

_____

**oo** _____

_____

**oe** _____

_____

**eo** _____

_____

**ow** _____

**ew** _____

_____

**eau** _____

**ou** _____

**oa** _____

_____

## SETTLING DIFFERENCES

Show the differences between the two words at the right by writing definitions for each. Put 'v' or 'n' in the boxes to show which is a verb and which is a noun. Circle the differing letters.

☐ **prophecy** _____

_____

☐ **prophesy** _____

_____

# LESSON 5

**TESTING...
TESTING...** Take your final test. Write your words in the spaces provided at the back of this book. Ask God to help you with your test.

# U NIT 6

# SPELLING 'U' SOUNDS

| | |
|---|---|
| slew | does |
| deuce | pullover |
| subdue | mistook |
| juice | woolen |
| viewpoint | bosom |
| bloodthirsty | woman |
| once | should |
| spongy | adieu |
| untouchable | scoop |
| young | beauty |

## LESSON 1

Study these list words, using the
study plan on page 7.

## LESSON 2        VOCABULARY / DICTIONARY

Use these list words in sentences. Consult a dictionary, if necessary, to understand their meanings. You may
use any tense (past, present, or future) of verbs, either singular or plural form of nouns, and comparative (-er)
or superlative (-est) forms of adjectives and adverbs, if you are careful to spell these alternative forms correctly.

**deuce** _____

_____

**slew** _____

_____

**spongy** _____

_____

**mistook** _____

_____

**bosom** _____

_____

**viewpoint** _____

_____

**subdue** _____

_____

# LESSON 3

## FOUNDATIONS

Write each of your list words three times on a separate sheet of paper.

## FINER THINGS

**1** Write a list word that fits best with the two words given.

1. loveliness, attractiveness _____

7. mushy, squishy _____

2. new, youthful _____

8. dig, gouge _____

3. overpower, conquer _____

9. opinion, outlook _____

4. lady, female _____

10. erred, misunderstood _____

5. violent, murderous _____

11. good-bye, farewell _____

6. murdered, butchered _____

12. chest, heart _____

**2** THE FRENCH CONNECTION

Write the two list words you see on the map of France at the right. These two English words have direct roots in the French language. Look up the words in an English dictionary and learn their meanings.

When the French say, "Adieu," they are literally saying: "to God." This way of saying "good-bye" originally was a short way of saying to a departing friend, "I commit you to God's care." The English word "good-bye" is a shortening of the phrase "God be with ye (you)," and therefore means nearly the same thing as the French "adieu" or the Spanish "adios," which also means "to God."

**deuce**

_____

**adieu**

_____

**3** Write the list words you find in these sentences.

1. The young woman held the child close to her bosom. _____ _____ _____

2. The bloodthristy fighters slew thousands in their attempt to subdue their enemies. _____

3. She wore a woolen pullover. _____ _____ _____

4. Once a thing of beauty, the rose was now wilted. _____

_____

5. That which he should do, he seldom does. _____ _____

24

## LESSON 4

Take your first practice test on all words in your Unit 6 word list. Write the words on a separate sheet of paper as they are read to you. Write any words you misspelled on your practice test five times on another sheet.

## WHAT'S IN A WORD?

Spellings for the long u sound = u, ew, ue, eu, ui, oo, ieu, iew, eau
Spellings for short u and other u sounds = u, o, ou, oo, oe
Write list words having these spellings of the 'u' sound.

**u** _____
_____
_____

**o** _____
_____
_____
_____

**ou** _____
_____
_____

**oo** _____
_____
_____

**ew** _____

**ue** _____

**eu** _____

**ui** _____

**ieu** _____

**iew** _____

**eau** _____

**oe** _____

## SETTLING DIFFERENCES

1. Which two-syllable list words have two u's?
Different sound/spelling ⤨ Same sound/different spelling

_____ _____

2. Write a two-syllable word with an 'o' in each syllable, each with a different 'u' sound.

_____

## LESSON 5

Take your final test. Write your words in the spaces provided at the back of this book. Ask God to help you with your test.

25

# UNIT 7

# SPELLING THE 'ER' SOUND

| | |
|---|---|
| verge | squirm |
| twirling | mirth |
| worldliness | worst |
| earthbound | wurst |
| hearse | pert |
| myrtle | journal |
| perfection | caliper |
| versify | caliber |
| dirge | squirrel |
| whirlwind | murder |

## LESSON 1

Study these list words, using the study plan on page 7.

## LESSON 2 — VOCABULARY / DICTIONARY

Use these list words in sentences. Consult a dictionary, if necessary, to understand their meanings. You may use any tense (past, present, or future) of verbs, either singular or plural form of nouns, and comparative (-er) or superlative (-est) forms of adjectives and adverbs, if you are careful to spell these alternative forms correctly.

**verge** _____

_____

**mirth** _____

_____

**dirge** _____

_____

**versify** _____

_____

**journal** _____

_____

**worldliness** _____

_____

**caliber** _____

_____

Write each of your list words three times on a separate sheet of paper.

## FINER THINGS

**1** Circle the letters in these two words that make their spellings different. Write the words and define them.

**caliber** _____ _____

_____

**caliper** _____ _____

_____

**2** Circle the letters in these two words that make their spellings different. Write the words and define them.

**worst** _____ _____

_____

**wurst** _____ _____

_____

**3** Write these two list words and their meanings. Consult a dictionary. Read Titus 2:11-13. What does this Bible verse say about worldliness?

**worldliness** _____ _____

_____

**earthbound** _____ _____

_____

## LESSON 4

Take your first practice test on all words in your Unit 7 word list. Write the words on a separate sheet of paper as they are read to you. Write any words you misspelled on your practice test five times on another sheet.

## WHAT'S IN A WORD?

Spellings for the 'er' sound = er, ir, or, ear, our, ur, yr
Write list words having these spellings of the 'er' sound.

**er** _____

_____

_____

_____

_____

_____

**or** _____

_____

**ur** _____

_____

**ear** _____

_____

**our** _____

**ir** _____

_____

_____

**yr** _____

### SETTLING DIFFERENCES

Which list word has two different spellings for the 'er' sound?

_____

_____

Read Hosea 8:7. What list word do you find?_____
What do you think the first half of this Bible verse means?

## LESSON 5

Take your final test. Write your words in the spaces provided at the back of this book. Begin and end your test with prayer.

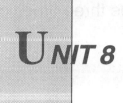

# U NIT 8

## SPELLING THE 'S' SOUND

| | |
|---|---|
| central | circuitous |
| sentinel | supersede |
| cistern | encyclopedia |
| cigarette | successive |
| cylinder | circumstance |
| citation | cyclical |
| synonym | sufferance |
| solemn | census |
| crosscut | consensus |
| cinema | cinnamon |

### LESSON 1

Study these list words, using the study plan on page 7.

### LESSON 2     VOCABULARY / DICTIONARY

Use these list words in sentences. Consult a dictionary, if necessary, to understand their meanings. You may use any tense (past, present, or future) of verbs, either singular or plural form of nouns, and comparative (-er) or superlative (-est) forms of adjectives and adverbs, if you are careful to spell these alternative forms correctly.

**circuitous** _____

_____

**cinema** _____

_____

**sentinel** _____

_____

**solemn** _____

_____

**supersede** _____

_____

**sufferance** _____

_____

**cistern** _____

_____

# LESSON 3

**FOUNDATIONS**     Write each of your list words three times on a separate sheet of paper.

**FINER THINGS**

**1**   Write all your list words in the spaces below. Circle every letter that spells the sound of 's.'

_____    _____    _____    _____

_____    _____    _____    _____

_____    _____    _____    _____

_____    _____    _____    _____

_____    _____    _____    _____

**2**   Write the two list words below. Examine the last six letters of the longer word. What difference do you find between these six letters and the six letters of the shorter word? Write the meaning of each word in the spaces.

**census** _____      **consensus** _____

_____      _____

_____      _____

**3**   Which list words are suggested by the words printed below?

**cigar** _____        **sense** _____

**circuit** _____        **suffer** _____

**cycle** _____        **succeed** _____

**cite** _____        **center** _____

30

# LESSON 4

Take your first practice test on all words in your Unit 8 word list. Write the words on a separate sheet of paper as they are read to you. Write any words you misspelled on your practice test five times on another sheet.

## WHAT'S IN A WORD?

Spellings for the 's' sound = s, ss, c (also sc, sch*)
Write list words having these spellings of the 's' sound.

**C**                    **S**                    **SS**

_____      _____      _____

_____      _____      _____

_____      _____      In which list words does
                                                  'c' have the sound of 'k'?
_____      _____

_____      _____      _____

_____      _____      _____

_____      _____      _____

_____      _____      _____

_____      _____      _____

_____

_____

*The 's' sound can also be spelled 'sc' as in 'scene,' 'scent,' 'scenario,' and 'scepter' or 'sch' as in 'schism.' None of your list words use this spelling.

### SPELLING/PHONICS RULE

When 'c' is followed immediately by 'e,' 'i,' or 'y,' it usually has the sound of 's' as in 'see.'
The consonant 'c' usually has the sound of 'k' unless it directly precedes 'e,' 'i,' 'y' and sometimes 'h.'

# LESSON 5

**TESTING... TESTING...**   Take your final test. Write your words in the spaces provided at the back of this book. Begin and end your test with prayer.

# U NIT 9

# SPELLING THE 'K' SOUND

| | |
|---|---|
| coward | chloride |
| coral | chlorinate |
| corral | antique |
| choral | croquet |
| chorale | croquette |
| crackling | sidekick |
| culprit | kickback |
| curry | kitchenette |
| Christlike | kiosk |
| chaotic | knapsack |

## *LESSON 1*

Study these list words, using the
study plan on page 7.

## *LESSON 2*      VOCABULARY / DICTIONARY

Use these list words in sentences. Consult a dictionary, if necessary, to understand their meanings. You may
use any tense (past, present, or future) of verbs, either singular or plural form of nouns, and comparative (-er)
or superlative (-est) forms of adjectives and adverbs, if you are careful to spell these alternative forms correctly.

**Christlike** _____

_____

**kiosk** _____

_____

**coward** _____

_____

**culprit** _____

_____

**sidekick** _____

_____

**kickback** _____

_____

**corral** _____

_____

# LESSON 3

Write each of your list words three times on a separate sheet of paper.

**FINER THINGS**

**1** Write these four list words. There are two sets of homonyms in this group. Draw lines connecting the homonyms.

**chorale** _____

**choral** _____

**coral** _____

**corral** _____

**2** Show that you know the differences in meaning of these words by writing a short definition of each. Use a dictionary, if necessary.

**chorale** _____

**choral** _____

**coral** _____

**corral** _____

**3** Which of the two words below goes with the picture? Circle the correct word. Write both words and define them.

**croquet** _____

_____

**croquette** _____

_____

**4** The suffix in the box below has three primary meanings. Write the two list words that have this suffix. Check which one of the three meanings applies to these list words. _____ _____

**-ette**

☐ small
*(dinette)*

☐ female
*(usherette)*

☐ imitation
*(leatherette)*

33

## LESSON 4

Take your first practice test on all words in your Unit 9 word list. Write the words on a separate sheet of paper as they are read to you. Write any words you misspelled on your practice test five times on another sheet.

## WHAT'S IN A WORD?

Spellings for the 'k' sound = k, c, ck, ch, qu
Write list words having these spellings of the 'k' sound.

**c**

_____

_____

_____

_____

_____

_____

_____

**ck**

_____

_____

_____

**ch**

_____

_____

_____

_____

_____

**k**

_____

_____

_____

**qu**

_____

_____

Which list word contains a letter 'k' that does NOT have the sound of 'k' as in 'kite'?

_____

Which list word has a 'ch' that does not have the sound of 'k' as in 'kite'?

Which list words have two different spellings for the 'k' sound?

_____  _____

_____  _____

_____  _____

_____

## LESSON 5

Take your final test. Write your words in the spaces provided at the back of this book. Begin and end your test with prayer.

34

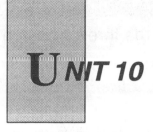

# UNIT 10

# SPELLING THE 'SH' SOUND

## LESSON 1

Study these list words, using the study plan on page 7.

| | |
|---|---|
| shudder | ferocious |
| shadow | magician |
| childish | socialism |
| charade | missionary |
| machinery | diversion |
| champagne | pension |
| cautious | confession |
| essential | sugar |
| petition | censure |
| deficient | pressure |

## LESSON 2 ▸ VOCABULARY / DICTIONARY

Use these list words in sentences. Consult a dictionary, if necessary, to understand their meanings. You may use any tense (past, present, or future) of verbs, either singular or plural form of nouns, and comparative (-er) or superlative (-est) forms of adjectives and adverbs, if you are careful to spell these alternative forms correctly.

**charade** _____

_____

**deficient** _____

_____

**socialism** _____

_____

**diversion** _____

_____

**censure** _____

_____

**essential** _____

_____

**ferocious** _____

_____

35

# LESSON 3

**FINER THINGS**

**1** Complete the list words below by writing the missing letters.

_____ery          _____ary

_____ious          _____ious

____ss_____          _____ss____

____ss_____          _____ss_____

**2** Complete the following sentences with list words. Choose from the words at the right; circle the correct word and write it in the blank.

| | |
|---|---|
| The voters signed a _____ to get their candidate on the ballot. | pension<br>petition<br>confession |
| The powerful wind caused the old house to _____ and the windows to rattle. | shadow<br>censure<br>shudder |
| Reading a novel can be a good _____ after a day of hard work. | diversion<br>petition<br>essential |
| The young pastor believed God had called him to become a _____ to central Africa. | magician<br>charade<br>missionary |
| Grandfather retired with a small _____ that was enough to allow him a comfortable living. | censure<br>pension<br>pressure |
| Andrew was crying, so his mother told him to stop being _____ and to act his age. | cautious<br>ferocious<br>childish |

# LESSON 4

## TAKING STOCK

Take your first practice test on all words in your Unit 10 word list. Write the words on a separate sheet of paper as they are read to you. Write any words you misspelled on your practice test five times on another sheet.

## WHAT'S IN A WORD?

Spellings for the 'sh' sound = sh, ch, ti, ci, si, su
Write list words having these spellings of the 'sh' sound.

**sh**

_____
_____
_____

**ch**

_____
_____
_____

**su**

_____
_____
_____

**ti**

_____
_____
_____

**ci**

_____
_____
_____

**si**

_____
_____
_____

Which list word has a 'ch' spelling that does not have the sound of 'sh'?

_____

Which list words go best with these pictures?

_____    _____

TESTING...
TESTING...

Take your final test. Write your words in the spaces provided at the back of this book. Begin and end your test with prayer.

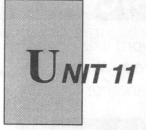

# U NIT 11

# TRICKY TRAILERS: -ar, -er, -or

| | |
|---|---|
| ancestor | debtor |
| secular | bachelor |
| coroner | instructor |
| author | calendar |
| tabular | nectar |
| straggler | conqueror |
| professor | similar |
| burglar | competitor |
| believer | rumor |
| governor | roomer |

## LESSON 1

Study these list words, using the study plan on page 7.

## LESSON 2    VOCABULARY / DICTIONARY

Use these list words in sentences. Consult a dictionary, if necessary, to understand their meanings. You may use any tense (past, present, or future) of verbs, either singular or plural form of nouns, and comparative (-er) or superlative (-est) forms of adjectives and adverbs, if you are careful to spell these alternative forms correctly.

**secular** _____

_____

**author** _____

_____

**straggler** _____

_____

**bachelor** _____

_____

**ancestor** _____

_____

**competitor** _____

_____

**nectar** _____

_____

# LESSON 3

Write each of your list words three times on a separate sheet of paper.

## FINER THINGS

**1** Unscramble these list words. Spell them correctly in the spaces.

| | | |
|---|---|---|
| **glarrub** | **stanroce** | **broted** |
| _____ | _____ | _____ |
| **chorleba** | **vornerog** | **quonerroc** |
| _____ | _____ | _____ |
| **regstralg** | **sorsropef** | **cotterpimo** |
| _____ | _____ | _____ |
| **cranet** | **ceusral** | **roonrec** |
| _____ | _____ | _____ |
| **limsira** | **rohtua** | **naclerad** |
| _____ | _____ | _____ |
| **murro** | **bratula** | **revebeli** |
| _____ | _____ | _____ |

**2** Find three list words among the letters in the box. Write the words.

| **eemmooooorrrrrrnuc** | _____ |
|---|---|
| | _____ |
| | _____ |

39

# LESSON 4

Take your first practice test on all words in your Unit 11 word list. Write the words on a separate sheet of paper as they are read to you. Write any words you misspelled on your practice test five times on another sheet.

## WHAT'S IN A WORD?

Tricky Trailers = -ar, -er, -or
Group and write list words with these endings

**ar**

**er**

**or**

_____   _____   _____

_____   _____   _____

_____   _____   _____

_____   _____   _____

_____                          _____

                                             _____

## —— ANTONYMS ——

                                             _____

                                             _____

Write list words that are antonyms for these words.

descendant_____        doubter_____

leader_____        student_____

partner_____         landlord_____

fact_____        different_____

sacred_____        creditor_____

# LESSON 5

Take your final test. Write your words in the spaces provided at the back of this book. Begin and end your test with prayer.

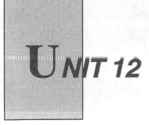

# UNIT 12

## TRICKY TRAILERS: -ar, -er, -or

| | |
|---|---|
| stagger | mortar |
| dipper | ledger |
| arbor | meteor |
| ardor | muscular |
| auditor | orator |
| bearer | mourner |
| lodger | traitor |
| captor | visitor |
| juror | surveyor |
| grocer | solar |

### LESSON 1

Study these list words, using the
study plan on page 7.

### LESSON 2        VOCABULARY / DICTIONARY

Use these list words in sentences. Consult a dictionary, if necessary, to understand their meanings. You may
use any tense (past, present, or future) of verbs, either singular or plural form of nouns, and comparative (-er)
or superlative (-est) forms of adjectives and adverbs, if you are careful to spell these alternative forms correctly.

**ardor** _____

_____

**captor** _____

_____

**muscular** _____

_____

**mourner** _____

_____

**orator** _____

_____

**bearer** _____

_____

**solar** _____

_____

# LESSON 3

**FOUNDATIONS** — Write each of your list words three times on a separate sheet of paper.

**FINER THINGS**

**1** Write list words that are suggested by these drawings of heavenly bodies.

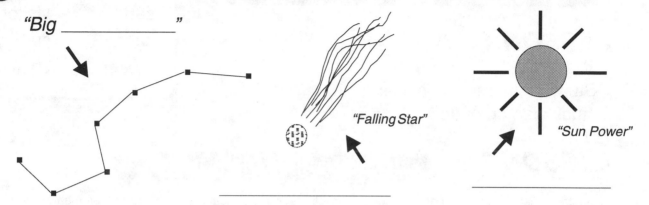

*"Big _____"*

*"Falling Star"*

*"Sun Power"*

_____

_____

**2** Supply the missing letters in these list words. Look up the words in a dictionary and write a short definition for each in the boxes.

## ar__or

## ar__or

**3** Without looking at your word list, circle the list word in these pairs. Write the circled word in the empty box.

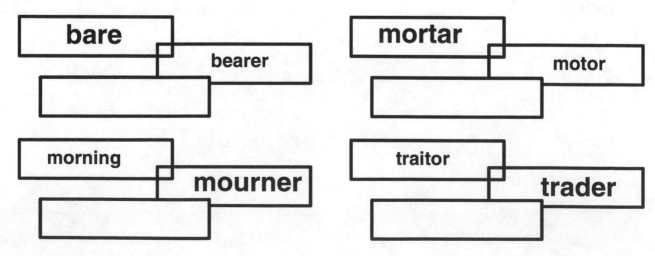

**bare**

bearer

**mortar**

motor

morning

**mourner**

traitor

**trader**

## LESSON 4

Take your first practice test on all words in your Unit 12 word list. Write the words on a separate sheet of paper as they are read to you. Write any words you misspelled on your practice test five times on another sheet.

### WHAT'S IN A WORD?

Tricky Trailers = -ar, -er, -or
Group and write list words with these endings

**er**                    **ar**                    **or**

_____          _____          _____

_____          _____          _____

_____          _____          _____

_____                                   _____

_____               _____

_____                                   _____

                                                  _____

                                                  _____

---

### Identify the following with list words:

One who mourns _____

One who surveys _____

One who gives orations _____

One who audits _____

One who bears things _____

One who betrays _____

One who visits _____

One who operates a grocery _____

One who lodges _____

One who sits on a jury _____

One who captures _____

**Fill in the blanks to make two list words. Define each word.**

l__dger: _____

_____

l__dger: _____

_____

## LESSON 5

Take your final test. Write your words in the spaces provided at the back of this book. Be sure to ask God for His blessing.

# UNIT 13

## TRICKY TRAILERS: -cal, -cle

| | |
|---|---|
| cubical | logical |
| cubicle | medical |
| muscle | critical |
| comical | spectacle |
| technical | magical |
| clerical | miracle |
| particle | typical |
| practical | receptacle |
| identical | obstacle |
| classical | vehicle |

### LESSON 1

Study these list words, using the study plan on page 7.

### LESSON 2

**VOCABULARY / DICTIONARY**

Use these list words in sentences. Consult a dictionary, if necessary, to understand their meanings. You may use any tense (past, present, or future) of verbs, either singular or plural form of nouns, and comparative (-er) or superlative (-est) forms of adjectives and adverbs, if you are careful to spell these alternative forms correctly.

**particle** _____

_____

**classical** _____

_____

**obstacle** _____

_____

**technical** _____

_____

**logical** _____

_____

**receptacle** _____

_____

**comical** _____

_____

# LESSON 3

## FOUNDATIONS

Write each of your list words three times on a separate sheet of paper.

## FINER THINGS

**1** Write your list words under the correct heading.

### SPELLING TIP

Words ending in '-cal' are usually adjectives.

Words ending in '-cle' are usually nouns.

**NOUNS**

_____

_____

_____

_____

_____

_____

_____

_____

**ADJECTIVES**

_____

_____

_____

_____

_____

_____

_____

_____

_____

_____

_____

_____

**2** Write the plural form of these list words.

| cubicle | spectacle | obstacle |
| particle | miracle | vehicle |
| muscle | receptacle | |

_____

_____

_____

_____

_____

_____

_____

_____

**3** Write the adverb form of these list words.

| comical | practical | logical | magical |
| technical | identical | medical | typical |
| clerical | classical | critical | cubical |

_____  _____

_____  _____

_____  _____

_____  _____

_____  _____

CLUES:  Nouns + s = plural
        Adjectives + ly = adverbs

45

## LESSON 4

Take your first practice test on all words in your Unit 13 word list. Write the words on a separate sheet of paper as they are read to you. Write any words you misspelled on your practice test five times on another sheet.

## WHAT'S IN A WORD?

Tricky Trailers = -cle, -cal
Group and write list words with these endings

### cal

_____
_____
_____
_____
_____
_____
_____
_____
_____
_____

### cle

_____
_____
_____
_____
_____
_____
_____

Complete these two list words:

cubic___ ___

cubic___ ___

**Write the answer:**

When Jesus raised the dead, was it [magical] or a [miracle]?

_____

If you were sick, would you prefer to see a [medical] doctor or a [vehicle] doctor?

_____

Do you prefer [classical] music or [comical] music?

_____

Would you place trash in a [receptacle] or in an [obstacle]?

_____

Do you move your arm with the help of a [muscle] or a [particle]?

_____

If twins are exactly alike, are they [typical] or [identical]?

_____

Unscramble these two list words:

partciel _____        particcla _____

## LESSON 5

Take your final test. Write your words in the spaces provided at the back of this book. Be sure to ask God for His blessing.

46

# U NIT 14

## TRICKY TRAILERS: -cy, -sy

| | |
|---|---|
| accuracy | tipsy |
| heresy | juicy |
| conspiracy | fallacy |
| controversy | fantasy |
| emergency | vacancy |
| hypocrisy | secrecy |
| tendency | privacy |
| decency | delicacy |
| embassy | policy |
| ecstasy | fleecy |

### LESSON 1

Study these list words, using the study plan on page 7.

### LESSON 2    VOCABULARY / DICTIONARY

Use these list words in sentences. Consult a dictionary, if necessary, to understand their meanings. You may use any tense (past, present, or future) of verbs, either singular or plural form of nouns, and comparative (-er) or superlative (-est) forms of adjectives and adverbs, if you are careful to spell these alternative forms correctly.

**vacancy** _____

_____

**secrecy** _____

_____

**privacy** _____

_____

**conspiracy** _____

_____

**policy** _____

_____

**controversy** _____

_____

**tendency** _____

_____

# LESSON 3

## FOUNDATIONS
Write each of your list words three times on a separate sheet of paper.

## FINER THINGS

**1** SPELLING DIFFERENT WORD FORMS. Fill in the blanks with list words.

**ADJECTIVE:** _accurate_

_decent_

_delicate_

_private_

_heretical_

_fantastic_

_secret_

_false_

_controversial_

**VERB:** _conspire_

_vacate_

_tend_

**NOUN:** _____

**2** Write list words that fit these situations.

| In Matthew 23 (New Testament part of the Bible), Jesus warns the Pharisees and scribes about saying one thing and doing something else or for acting one way on the outside but being something else on the inside. He is pronouncing judgment upon them for a particular sin. | An accident happens in your home while your parents are gone. Some one is hurt and you need help. So you go to the telephone and call 9-1-1, a special number where an expert will help you get in touch with the police, fire department or ambulance company. | Your family is traveling across the country on vacation. You are all tired and decide to stop at a motel for the night. All of the motels you see have a sign out front telling you there are no rooms available. Finally you see a sign that makes you happy. It shows there is still room inside. |
|---|---|---|
| _____ | _____ | _____ |

## LESSON 4

Take your first practice test on all words in your Unit 14 word list. Write the words on a separate sheet of paper as they are read to you. Write any words you misspelled on your practice test five times on another sheet.

## WHAT'S IN A WORD?

Tricky Trailers = -cy, -sy
Group and write list words with these endings

**cy**

_____

_____

_____

_____

_____

_____

_____

_____

_____

_____

_____

**sy**

_____

_____

_____

_____

_____

_____

_____

_____

_____

_____

_____

**Write the answer:**

Is a false teaching a [policy] or a [heresy]?

_____

If a piece of fruit contains a lot of liquid, is it [fleecy] or [juicy]?

_____

If you try to spell your words correctly, are you striving for [delicacy] or [accuracy]?

_____

Is your country's chief office in another nation a [conspiracy] or an [embassy]?

_____

Are the school rules the official [policy] or [heresy]?

_____

Show that you know the differences in meaning of 'privacy,' 'secrecy,' and 'conspiracy' by writing short definitions in the box.

## LESSON 5

**TESTING... TESTING...**

Take your final test. Write your words in the spaces provided at the back of this book. Be sure to ask God for His blessing.

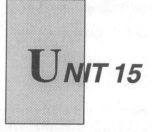

# UNIT 15

# TRICKY TRAILERS:-ise, -ize, -yze

| | |
|---|---|
| baptize | advertise |
| enterprise | civilize |
| legalize | idolize |
| chastise | moralize |
| merchandise | criticize |
| compromise | comprise |
| paralyze | despise |
| recognize | devise |
| supervise | improvise |
| memorize | analyze |

## LESSON 1

Study these list words, using the study plan on page 7.

## LESSON 2 VOCABULARY/DICTIONARY

Use these list words in sentences. Consult a dictionary, if necessary, to understand their meanings. You may use any tense (past, present, or future) of verbs, either singular or plural form of nouns, and comparative (-er) or superlative (-est) forms of adjectives and adverbs, if you are careful to spell these alternative forms correctly.

**recognize** _____

_____

**idolize** _____

_____

**despise** _____

_____

**criticize** _____

_____

**chastise** _____

_____

**compromise** _____

_____

**merchandise** _____

_____

# LESSON 3

## FOUNDATIONS

Write each of your list words three times on a separate sheet of paper.

## FINER THINGS

**1** Write the words given in each column. Follow the same pattern for the other words in each group.

| | |
|---|---|
| baptize _____ | baptism _____ |
| legalize _____ | ⟶ _____ |
| moralize _____ | ⟶ _____ |
| criticize _____ | ⟶ _____ |
| | |
| civilize _____ | civilization _____ |
| improvise _____ | ⟶ _____ |
| idolize _____ | ⟶ _____ |
| | |
| paralyze _____ | paralysis _____ |
| analyze _____ | ⟶ _____ |
| | |
| chastise _____ | chastisement _____ |
| advertise _____ | ⟶ _____ |

**2** Write:                     Insert two letters
                                 to spell another
                                 list word:
comprise _____         _____

**3** Write these two words.
Look them up in a dictionary     devise _____
and learn their different meanings.     device _____

51

## LESSON 4

Take your first practice test on all words in your Unit 15 word list. Write the words on a separate sheet of paper as they are read to you. Write any words you misspelled on your practice test five times on another sheet.

## WHAT'S IN A WORD?

Tricky Trailers = -ise, -ize, -yze
Group and write list words with these endings

### ise

_____
_____
_____
_____
_____
_____
_____
_____
_____

### ize

_____
_____
_____
_____
_____
_____
_____

### yze

_____
_____

**Write these list words and learn to tell the difference.**

**chastise**     **criticize**     **despise**

_____  _____  _____

### Write the answer:

If I make something up, do I [memorize] or [improvise] it?

_____

To sell your product, would it be better to [advertise] it or [criticize] it?

_____

If you wanted to make something lawful, would you [despise] it or [legalize] it?

_____

If John started a business, would it be called his [enterprise] or his [merchandise]?

_____

Would the items sold in John's business be his [enterprise] or his [merchandise]?

_____

Is it better to [recognize] your heroes or to [idolize] them?

_____

## LESSON 5

TESTING...
TESTING...

Take your final test. Write your words in the spaces provided at the back of this book. Seek God's help through prayer.

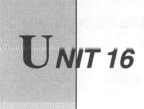

# UNIT 16

## TRICKY TRAILERS: -able, -ible

| | |
|---|---|
| visible | accessible |
| deplorable | respectable |
| reversible | audible |
| receivable | durable |
| suitable | digestible |
| tangible | infallible |
| responsible | credible |
| permissible | advisable |
| acceptable | susceptible |
| available | applicable |

### LESSON 1

Study these list words, using the study plan on page 7.

### LESSON 2    VOCABULARY / DICTIONARY

Use these list words in sentences. Consult a dictionary, if necessary, to understand their meanings. You may use any tense (past, present, or future) of verbs, either singular or plural form of nouns, and comparative (-er) or superlative (-est) forms of adjectives and adverbs, if you are careful to spell these alternative forms correctly.

**audible** _____

_____

**visible** _____

_____

**tangible** _____

_____

**respectable** _____

_____

**credible** _____

_____

**suitable** _____

_____

**permissible** _____

_____

# LESSON 3

## FOUNDATIONS

Write each of your list words three times on a separate sheet of paper.

## FINER THINGS

**1** Write list words to fit the clues.

**"Able to be believed"**

**"Able to be heard"**

**"Able to be seen"**

**"Able to be touched"**

**"Able to be digested"**

**2** Write adjectives from your word list that are suggested by these nouns and verbs.

vision _____

respond _____

deplore _____

permit _____

apply _____

respect _____

reverse _____

receive _____

access _____

suit _____

endure _____

avail _____

advise _____

accept _____

digest _____

creed _____

fallacy _____

audio _____

54

## LESSON 4

Take your first practice test on all words in your Unit 16 word list. Write the words on a separate sheet of paper as they are read to you. Write any words you misspelled on your practice test five times on another sheet.

## WHAT'S IN A WORD?

Tricky Trailers = -able, -ible
Group and write list words with these endings

**able**

**ible**

_____

_____

_____

_____

_____

_____

_____

_____

Write the words below and draw lines between the words on the left that go best with words on the right.

| | | | |
|---|---|---|---|
| _____ | **permissible** | **receivable** | _____ |
| _____ | **available** | **suitable** | _____ |
| _____ | **applicable** | **acceptable** | _____ |

## Infallible

Write the word above in the blank.

*Only God and His Word are infallible. Read the statement below and learn what it means.*

"Holy Scripture, being God's own Word, written by men prepared and superintended by His Spirit, is of infallible divine authority in all matters upon which it touches: it is to be believed, as God's instruction, in all that it affirms; obeyed, as God's command, in all that it requires; embraced, as God's pledge, in all that it promises.

"The Holy Spirit, Scripture's Divine Author, both authenticates it to us by His inward witness and opens our minds to understand its meaning.

"Being wholly and verbally God-given, Scripture is without error or fault in all its teaching...."

*From the Chicago Statement on Biblical Inerrancy*

## LESSON 5

Take your final test. Write your words in the spaces provided at the back of this book. Seek God's help through prayer.

# UNIT 17

## TRICKY TRAILERS: -eous, -ious

| | |
|---|---|
| hideous | religious |
| courteous | sacrilegious |
| righteous | outrageous |
| gorgeous | spontaneous |
| copious | simultaneous |
| dubious | instantaneous |
| gaseous | miscellaneous |
| aqueous | amphibious |
| delirious | impervious |
| erroneous | pretentious |

### LESSON 1

Study these list words, using the study plan on page 7.

### LESSON 2

**VOCABULARY / DICTIONARY**

Use these list words in sentences. Consult a dictionary, if necessary, to understand their meanings. You may use any tense (past, present, or future) of verbs, either singular or plural form of nouns, and comparative (-er) or superlative (-est) forms of adjectives and adverbs, if you are careful to spell these alternative forms correctly.

**gorgeous** _____

_____

**hideous** _____

_____

**religious** _____

_____

**sacrilegious** _____

_____

**copious** _____

_____

**delirious** _____

_____

**outrageous** _____

_____

# LESSON 3

Write each of your list words three times on a separate sheet of paper.

## FINER THINGS

**1** CONTRASTS. Write these list words. Look them up in your dictionary and write a brief definition for each.

| hideous | gorgeous |
|---------|----------|
|         |          |
|         |          |
|         |          |
|         |          |
|         |          |
|         |          |
|         |          |

| righteous | erroneous |
|-----------|-----------|
|           |           |
|           |           |
|           |           |
|           |           |
|           |           |
|           |           |
|           |           |

| religious | sacrilegious |
|-----------|--------------|
|           |              |
|           |              |
|           |              |
|           |              |
|           |              |
|           |              |
|           |              |

| gaseous | aqueous |
|---------|---------|
|         |         |
|         |         |
|         |         |
|         |         |
|         |         |
|         |         |
|         |         |

**2** Write adjectives from your word list that are derived from these words.

gas _____          instant _____

religion _____     pretense _____

right _____        doubt _____

courtesy _____     error _____

outrage _____

## LESSON 4

Take your first practice test on all words in your Unit 17 word list. Write the words on a separate sheet of paper as they are read to you. Write any words you misspelled on your practice test five times on another sheet.

## WHAT'S IN A WORD?

Tricky Trailers = -eous, -ious
Group and write list words with these endings

### eous

_____
_____
_____
_____
_____
_____
_____
_____
_____
_____

### ious

_____
_____
_____
_____
_____
_____

**Study the diagram below. Write the two list words.**

**religious**

✗

**sacrilegious**

_____
_____

*"...the righteous Lord loveth righteousness."*

Psalm 11:7

---

Write these list words. Circle the best synonym.

**delirious**
_____
a. neglectful
b. crazy
c. suspicious

**spontaneous**
_____
a. impulsive
b. fine
c. weird

**sacrilegious**
_____
a. holy
b. harmful
c. profane

**impervious**
_____
a. watertight
b. remarkable
c. essential

## LESSON 5

Take your final test. Write your words in the spaces provided at the back of this book. Seek God's help through prayer.

# UNIT 18

## TRICKY TRAILERS: -ant, -ent

| | |
|---|---|
| assailant | dependent |
| arrogant | combatant |
| stagnant | descendant |
| vigilant | expedient |
| vagrant | competent |
| inclement | triumphant |
| reluctant | conversant |
| insolvent | despondent |
| recipient | correspondent |
| prevalent | consistent |

### LESSON 1

Study these list words, using the study plan on page 7.

### LESSON 2    VOCABULARY / DICTIONARY

Use these list words in sentences. Consult a dictionary, if necessary, to understand their meanings. You may use any tense (past, present, or future) of verbs, either singular or plural form of nouns, and comparative (-er) or superlative (-est) forms of adjectives and adverbs, if you are careful to spell these alternative forms correctly.

**competent** _____

_____

**recipient** _____

_____

**triumphant** _____

_____

**reluctant** _____

_____

**stagnant** _____

_____

**consistent** _____

_____

**descendant** _____

_____

# LESSON 3

Write each of your list words three times on a separate sheet of paper.

**FINER THINGS**

**1** The list words below may be used either as nouns or adjectives. Write the words. Consult a dictionary and write both noun and adjective definitions.

| | NOUN | ADJECTIVE |
|---|---|---|
| **dependent** | | |
| **vagrant** | | |
| **expedient** | | |
| **correspondent** | | |
| **recipient** | | |
| **combatant** | | |
| **insolvent** | | |

**2** The list word 'descendant' is a noun. It may also be an adjective, but when it is an adjective, it is <u>usually</u> spelled 'descendent.' Write the list word, spelling it as a noun. Look for the two spellings in a dictionary, and study the differences in meanings.

**3** All other list words are adjectives, except 'assailant,' which is a _____.

## LESSON 4

Take your first practice test on all words in your Unit 18 word list. Write the words on a separate sheet of paper as they are read to you. Write any words you misspelled on your practice test five times on another sheet.

## WHAT'S IN A WORD?

Tricky Trailers = -ant, -ent
Group and write list words with these endings

**ant**                    **ent**

_____          _____

_____          _____

_____          _____

_____          _____

_____          _____

_____          _____

_____          _____

_____          _____

Write these list words. Circle the best synonym.

**assailant**
_____
a. assistant
b. enemy
c. sailor

**insolvent**
_____
a. bankrupt
b. influenced
c. inconsistent

**prevalent**
_____
a. former
b. widespread
c. secluded

| **triumphant** | **expedient** | **inclement** | **despondent** |
|---|---|---|---|
| _____ | _____ | _____ | _____ |
| a. alarming | a. useful | a. ceaseless | a. demolished |
| b. victorious | b. explosive | b. unproductive | b. detached |
| c. traditional | c. expensive | c. stormy | c. discouraged |

## LESSON 5

 TESTING... TESTING...

Take your final test. Write your words in the spaces provided at the back of this book. Study and prayer mean success.

61

# U NIT 19

# TRICKY TRAILERS: -cious, -tious

| | |
|---|---|
| judicious | superstitious |
| malicious | suspicious |
| nutritious | ostentatious |
| vicious | contentious |
| infectious | conscientious |
| tenacious | conscious |
| precious | factious |
| precocious | facetious |
| pernicious | factitious |
| vexatious | fictitious |

## LESSON 1

Study these list words, using the study plan on page 7.

## LESSON 2     VOCABULARY / DICTIONARY

Use these list words in sentences. Consult a dictionary, if necessary, to understand their meanings. You may use any tense (past, present, or future) of verbs, either singular or plural form of nouns, and comparative (-er) or superlative (-est) forms of adjectives and adverbs, if you are careful to spell these alternative forms correctly.

**suspicious** _____

_____

**vicious** _____

_____

**precious** _____

_____

**superstitious** _____

_____

**conscious** _____

_____

**nutritious** _____

_____

**malicious** _____

_____

# LESSON 3

## FOUNDATIONS
Write each of your list words three times on a separate sheet of paper.

## FINER THINGS

**1** Spell these three list words.

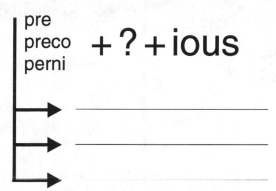

pre
preco
perni
+ ? + ious

→ _____

→ _____

→ _____

**2** Spell these three list words.

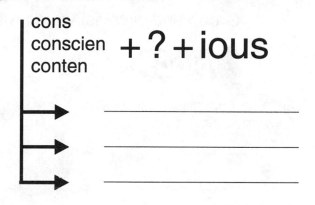

cons
conscien
conten
+ ? + ious

→ _____

→ _____

→ _____

**3** Spell these four list words.

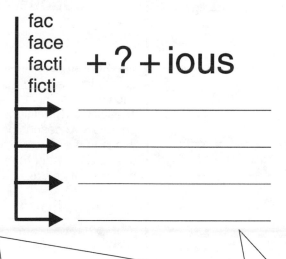

fac
face
facti
ficti
+ ? + ious

→ _____

→ _____

→ _____

→ _____

a. careful, reliable
b. artificial
c. annoying
d. quarrelsome
e. skillful at a young age
f. spiteful, hateful
g. sensible, well-advised
h. divisive, partisan
i. humorous, playful
j. holding firmly, or persistent
k. very harmful, or destructive
l. showy, lavishly displayed

**4** Write these list words. Select the correct definition by writing its letter in the blank. Choose from the arrow at bottom, left.

___ ostentatious _____

___ pernicious _____

___ tenacious _____

___ precocious _____

___ vexatious _____

___ contentious _____

___ factitious _____

___ judicious _____

___ factious _____

___ malicious _____

___ facetious _____

___ conscientious _____

# LESSON 4

Take your first practice test on all words in your Unit 19 word list. Write the words on a separate sheet of paper as they are read to you. Write any words you misspelled on your practice test five times on another sheet.

## WHAT'S IN A WORD?

Tricky Trailers = -cious, -tious
Group and write list words with these endings

### cious

_____
_____
_____
_____
_____
_____
_____
_____

### tious

_____
_____
_____
_____
_____
_____
_____
_____

All of your Unit 19 list words are adjectives. Which list words are related to the nouns and verbs given below?

faction _____

judge _____

fiction _____

suspect _____

contend _____

infect _____

conscience _____

---

Write these list words. Study and understand the history of the words.

### factious

_____

The English word 'factious' comes from a Latin word, 'factio,' meaning 'faction,' or a self-seeking part of a larger group. The list word 'factious' is an adjective describing such a party.

### factitious

_____

The English word 'factitious' comes from a Latin word, 'facare,' meaning 'to make.' The list word 'factitious' is an adjective describing things that are man-made or artificial, rather than products of nature.

### facetious

_____

'Facetious' comes from a Latin word, 'facetia,' meaning 'jest.' The list word, 'facetious' is an adjective describing actions or words that are done or said in jest or in a joking, witty manner.

# LESSON 5

TESTING...
    TESTING...

Take your final test. Write your words in the spaces provided at the back of this book. Study and prayer mean success.

# U NIT 20

## TRICKY TRAILERS: -ance, -ence

| | |
|---|---|
| existence | compliance |
| annoyance | obedience |
| innocence | occurrence |
| vengeance | nuisance |
| violence | maintenance |
| essence | intelligence |
| diligence | residence |
| reverence | repentance |
| alliance | appearance |
| fragrance | deliverance |

### LESSON 1

Study these list words, using the
study plan on page 7.

### LESSON 2

**VOCABULARY / DICTIONARY**

Use these list words in sentences. Consult a dictionary, if necessary, to understand their meanings. You may use any tense (past, present, or future) of verbs, either singular or plural form of nouns, and comparative (-er) or superlative (-est) forms of adjectives and adverbs, if you are careful to spell these alternative forms correctly.

**innocence** _____

_____

**reverence** _____

_____

**obedience** _____

_____

**residence** _____

_____

**nuisance** _____

_____

**fragrance** _____

_____

**alliance** _____

_____

# LESSON 3

## FOUNDATIONS
Write each of your list words three times on a separate sheet of paper.

## FINER THINGS

**1** Spell these list words correctly.

exist + ? + nce          _____

annoy + ? + nce          _____

repent + ? + nce         _____

appear + ? + nce         _____

deliver + ? + nce        _____

**2** Change these verbs into list words that are nouns.

comply _____        reside _____

obey _____          occur _____

revere _____        ally _____

**3** Which list words are related to these words?

revenge _____

diligent _____

fragrant _____

violate _____

maintain _____

intelligent _____

essential _____

innocent _____

**Write the list words you find in these phrases:**

*"reverence for God"*

_____

*"obedience to parents"*

_____

*"repentance for sins"*

_____

*"the appearance of evil"*

_____

*"deliverance from death"*

_____

*"compliance with rules"*

_____

66

Take your first practice test on all words in your Unit 20 word list. Write the words on a separate sheet of paper as they are read to you. Write any words you misspelled on your practice test five times on another sheet.

## WHAT'S IN A WORD?

Tricky Trailers = -ance, -ence
Group and write list words with these endings

**ance**

_____
_____
_____
_____
_____
_____
_____
_____

**ence**

_____
_____
_____
_____
_____
_____
_____
_____

### Write these list words. Circle the best synonym.

**essence**

_____

a. character
b. respect
c. health

**diligence**

_____

a. hospitality
b. earnestness
c. inability

**fragrance**

_____

a. frequence
b. outrage
c. aroma

**maintenance**

_____

a. preservation
b. government
c. organization

### Pair words from Group A with words from Group B by writing them in connecting boxes.

**A**

existence
annoyance
innocence
vengeance
compliance

**B**

repentance
nuisance
violence
obedience
essence

# LESSON 5

**TESTING...**
**TESTING...**

Take your final test. Write your words in the spaces provided at the back of this book. Ask God to help you spell correctly.

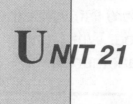

# UNIT 21

## A, E, OR I

| | |
|---|---|
| celebrate | ornament |
| supplement | revenue |
| implement | tragedy |
| liquefy | serenade |
| privilege | secretary |
| prodigal | apathy |
| petroleum | academy |
| skeleton | cataract |
| separate | salary |
| almanac | celery |

### LESSON 1

Study these list words, using the study plan on page 7.

### LESSON 2 — VOCABULARY / DICTIONARY

Use these list words in sentences. Consult a dictionary, if necessary, to understand their meanings. You may use any tense (past, present, or future) of verbs, either singular or plural form of nouns, and comparative (-er) or superlative (-est) forms of adjectives and adverbs, if you are careful to spell these alternative forms correctly.

**ornament** _____

_____

**academy** _____

_____

**celebrate** _____

_____

**privilege** _____

_____

**tragedy** _____

_____

**skeleton** _____

_____

**supplement** _____

_____

# LESSON 3

## FOUNDATIONS

Write each of your list words three times on a separate sheet of paper.

## FINER THINGS

**1** Spell these list words correctly.

| | | | |
|---|---|---|---|
| cel + ? + brate | _____ | trag + ? + dy | _____ |
| prod + ? + gal | _____ | cat + ? + ract | _____ |
| orn + ? + ment | _____ | liqu + ? + fy | _____ |
| ap + ? + thy | _____ | sep + ? + rate | _____ |
| suppl + ? + ment | _____ | ser + ? + nade | _____ |
| petrol + ? + um | _____ | sal + ? + ry | _____ |
| rev + ? + nue | _____ | priv + ? + lege | _____ |
| acad + ? + my | _____ | alm + ? + nac | _____ |
| impl + ? + ment | _____ | secr + ? + tary | _____ |
| skel + ? + ton | | cel + ? + ry | _____ |

**2** Complete these list words.

| | | | |
|---|---|---|---|
| _____ | ele | _____ | _____ ala _____ |
| _____ | ele | _____ | _____ ata _____ |
| _____ | ele | _____ | _____ ana _____ |
| _____ | ere | _____ | _____ ara _____ |
| _____ | eve | _____ | _____ ara _____ |
| _____ | ege | | _____ aca _____ |
| _____ | eme | _____ | _____ apa _____ |
| _____ | eme | _____ | _____ ivi _____ |

**3**

**TAKE NOTE**

a. liqu ⓘ d ⟶ liqu ⓔ fy. Write: 'liquefy' _____

b. To 'separate' is to break into 'parts': sePARaTe.
Write: 'separate' _____

c. Write these words. Learn the differences in meaning. { celery _____
{ salary _____

69

# LESSON 4

Take your first practice test on all words in your Unit 21 word list. Write the words on a separate sheet of paper as they are read to you. Write any words you misspelled on your practice test five times on another sheet.

## WHAT'S IN A WORD?

Except for 'petroleum' and 'academy,' the words in this unit's list are most often mispelled by using the wrong vowel in the second syllable. This is because common pronunciation fails to clearly distinguish the sound of the vowels 'a,' 'e,' or 'i' in these syllables. The same problem occurs in the third syllable of 'petroleum' and 'academy.'

Write these list words:

**petroleum**                    **academy**

_____    _____

Group the rest of your list words according to the vowels in the second syllables.

**e**                             **a**

_____    _____

_____    _____

_____    _____

_____    _____

_____    _____

_____    **i**

_____    _____

_____

---

Write these list words. Circle the best synonym.

**prodigal**

_____

a. wasteful
b. wicked
c. fun-loving

**serenade**

_____

a. gossip
b. quietness
c. melody

**cataract**

_____

a. waterfall
b. sailboat
c. automobile

**implement**

_____

a. fingerprint
b. device
c. continuation

---

# LESSON 5

Take your final test. Write your words in the spaces provided at the back of this book. Ask God to help you with your test.

# U*NIT 22*

## C, S, OR SC

| | |
|---|---|
| ascertain | intercede |
| scepter | scenic |
| descend | romance |
| crescent | porcelain |
| diverse | fluorescent |
| eclipse | coincidence |
| rescind | eloquence |
| scenery | necessary |
| transcend | docile |
| lettuce | decimal |

## *LESSON 1*

Study these list words, using the study plan on page 7.

## *LESSON 2*  VOCABULARY / DICTIONARY

Use these list words in sentences. Consult a dictionary, if necessary, to understand their meanings. You may use any tense (past, present, or future) of verbs, either singular or plural form of nouns, and comparative (-er) or superlative (-est) forms of adjectives and adverbs, if you are careful to spell these alternative forms correctly.

**descend** _____

_____

**lettuce** _____

_____

**necessary** _____

_____

**intercede** _____

_____

**porcelain** _____

_____

**scenery** _____

_____

**fluorescent** _____

_____

# LESSON 3

## FOUNDATIONS

Write each of your list words three times on a separate sheet of paper.

## FINER THINGS

**1** Write all list words with the 'sc' consonant digraph.

_____     _____

_____     _____

_____     _____

_____     _____

_____

**2** Write all list words that use a 'soft c' to spell the sound of 's' as in 'sin.'

_____     _____

_____     _____

_____     _____

_____     _____

_____

**3** Write all list words that use an 's' or 'double-s' to spell the sound of 's' as in 'sin.'

_____

_____

_____

*scenery   scenic*

Which of the two words above is an adjective?

_____

Which of the two words is a noun?

_____

The list word 'eloquence' is often confused with another word that looks and sounds similar. Do the exercise below to help learn the difference. (NOTE: The word 'elegance' is not a list word.)

**4**

*eloquence   elegance*

Which of the two words above best describes grace and refinement in appearance, movement or manners?

_____

Which of the two words best describes grace and persuasiveness in speech or gesture?

_____

*transcend   descend*

Which of the two words above means 'to move beyond'?

_____

Which of the two words means 'to move down'?

_____

# LESSON 4

Take your first practice test on all words in your Unit 22 word list. Write the words on a separate sheet of paper as they are read to you. Write any words you misspelled on your practice test five times on another sheet.

## WHAT'S IN A WORD?

### C, S, OR SC
Complete these list words.

a _____ ertain

coin _____ iden _____ e

de _____ end

cre _____ ent

diver _____ e

ne _____ e _____ ary

re _____ ind

_____ enery

tran _____ end

lettu _____ e

inter _____ ede

_____ enic

roman _____ e

por _____ elain

fluore _____ ent

_____ epter

eloquen _____ e

eclip _____ e

do _____ ile

de _____ imal

Choose list words to fit the clues.

"fine dishes" _____

"bright color" _____

"symbol of royal authority" _____

"quarter-moon" _____

### Write these list words. Circle the best synonym.

**docile**

_____

a. tame
b. cursed
c. medical

**rescind**

_____

a. announce
b. void
c. remark

**intercede**

_____

a. pray for
b. long for
c. give in

**ascertain**

_____

a. prepare
b. arrest
c. discover, learn

# LESSON 5

Take your final test. Write your words in the spaces provided at the back of this book. Ask God to help you with your test.

73

# U NIT 23

## SUFFIX RULE ONE

| | |
|---|---|
| advisable | guided |
| adoring | valuable |
| plagued | stylish |
| grieving | virtuous |
| obliged | salable |
| recyclable | admirer |
| roguish | desirable |
| curable | bluish |
| achieving | erasable |
| deceased | excusable |

### LESSON 1

Study these list words, using the study plan on page 7.

### LESSON 2     VOCABULARY / DICTIONARY

Use these list words in sentences. Consult a dictionary, if necessary, to understand their meanings. You may use any tense (past, present, or future) of verbs, either singular or plural form of nouns, and comparative (-er) or superlative (-est) forms of adjectives and adverbs, if you are careful to spell these alternative forms correctly.

**adoring** _____

_____

**grieving** _____

_____

**curable** _____

_____

**virtuous** _____

_____

**desirable** _____

_____

**achieving** _____

_____

**recyclable** _____

_____

# LESSON 3

## FOUNDATIONS

Write each of your list words three times on a separate sheet of paper.

## FINER THINGS

---

**SUFFIX RULE ONE**
Final 'e' is dropped from a root word before adding a suffix beginning with a vowel.

---

**1** Add the suffixes shown to these words.

|  | -ed | -ing | -able | -er |
|---|---|---|---|---|
| admire | _____ | _____ | _____ | _____ |
| advise | _____ | _____ | _____ | _____ |
| adore | _____ | _____ | _____ | _____ |
| erase | _____ | _____ | _____ | _____ |
| recycle | _____ | _____ | _____ | _____ |

**2** Add the suffixes shown to these words.

|  | -ed | -ing | -able |
|---|---|---|---|
| desire | _____ | _____ | _____ |
| excuse | _____ | _____ | _____ |
| value | _____ | _____ | _____ |
| achieve | _____ | _____ | _____ |
| cure | _____ | _____ | _____ |

**rogue**
An unprincipled person; a scamp; a scoundrel

**-ish**
Having the nature or character of

*Write: roguish*

_____

**3** Add the suffixes shown to these words.

|  | -ed | -ing |
|---|---|---|
| plague | _____ | _____ |
| guide | _____ | _____ |
| grieve | _____ | _____ |
| oblige | _____ | _____ |

| *plague-* | To harass; to afflict with calamity | *Write: plagued* |
| *plaque-* | A flat piece used for decoration or inscription; a tooth disease | _____ |

**4** Add the suffixes shown to to these words.

| rogue + ish | _____ |
| blue + ish | _____ |
| style + ish | _____ |
| style + ed | _____ |
| style + ing | _____ |
| virtue + ous | _____ |
| sale + able | _____ |

75

## LESSON 4

Take your first practice test on all words in your Unit 23 word list. Write the words on a separate sheet of paper as they are read to you. Write any words you misspelled on your practice test five times on another sheet.

## WHAT'S IN A WORD?

Write all list words with this suffix: '-able.'

_____    _____
_____    _____
_____    _____
_____    _____

Write all list words with this suffix: '-ed.'

_____    _____
_____    _____

Write all list words with this suffix: '-ing.'

_____    _____
_____

Write all list words with this suffix: '-ish.'

_____    _____
_____

Write a list word with this suffix: '-ous.'

_____

Write a list word with this suffix: '-er.'

_____

### Write these list words. Circle the best synonym.

**virtuous**

_____

a. upright
b. powerful
c. lively

**obliged**

_____

a. hidden
b. haunted
c. required

**salable**

_____

a. safeguarded
b. marketable
c. remarkable

**grieving**

_____

a. grunting
b. crushing
c. sorrowing

## LESSON 5

 TESTING...
TESTING...

Take your final test. Write your words in the spaces provided at the back of this book. Ask God to help you with your test.

# U *NIT 24*

## SUFFIX RULE TWO

| | |
|---|---|
| swimming | forgotten |
| drummer | ragged |
| squatter | clannish |
| equipping | allotted |
| acquitted | starry |
| unfitting | throbbing |
| referred | stirring |
| occurring | shopping |
| regretted | thinnest |
| admitted | gladden |

### LESSON 1

Study these list words, using the
study plan on page 7.

### LESSON 2 — VOCABULARY / DICTIONARY

Use these list words in sentences. Consult a dictionary, if necessary, to understand their meanings. You may
use any tense (past, present, or future) of verbs, either singular or plural form of nouns, and comparative (-er)
or superlative (-est) forms of adjectives and adverbs, if you are careful to spell these alternative forms correctly.

**forgotten** _____

_____

**throbbing** _____

_____

**gladden** _____

_____

**unfitting** _____

_____

**acquitted** _____

_____

**admitted** _____

_____

**starry** _____

_____

# LESSON 3

## FOUNDATIONS

Write each of your list words three times on a separate sheet of paper.

## FINER THINGS

---

### SUFFIX RULE TWO

In one-syllable words and in words accented on the last syllable, a final consonant after a single vowel is doubled before a suffix beginning with a vowel is added. (Final consonants 'x,' 'k,' and 'v' are never doubled.)

---

**1** Combine these root words and suffixes to spell list words.

throb + ing _____          occur + ing _____

forgot + en _____          squat + er _____

unfit + ing _____          thin + est _____

swim + ing _____          allot + ed _____

stir + ing _____          regret + ed _____

rag + ed _____          equip + ing _____

refer + ed _____          glad + en _____

drum + er _____          star + y _____

shop + ing _____          admit + ed _____

clan + ish _____          acquit + ed _____

**2** Write a list word that belongs with each group.

| | | |
|---|---|---|
| hiking<br>picnicking<br>camping<br><br>_____ | sadden<br>delight<br>please<br><br>_____ | sunny<br>cloudy<br>hazy<br><br>_____ |
| fattest<br>slimmest<br>skinniest<br><br>_____ | buying<br>purchasing<br>exchanging<br><br>_____ | erased<br>lost<br>absent<br><br>_____ |

78

# LESSON 4

Take your first practice test on all words in your Unit 24 word list. Write the words on a separate sheet of paper as they are read to you. Write any words you misspelled on your practice test five times on another sheet.

## WHAT'S IN A WORD?

Write all list words with this suffix: '-ing.'

_____    _____
_____    _____
_____    _____

Write all list words with this suffix: '-ed.'

_____    _____
_____    _____
_____    _____

Write all list words with this suffix: '-er.'

_____    _____

Write all list words with this suffix: '-en.'

_____    _____

Write a list word with          Write a list word with
this suffix: '-ish.'            this suffix: '-est.'

_____    _____

Write a list word with
this suffix: '-y.'

_____

---

**Write these list words. Circle the best synonym.**

**clannish**

_____

a. group-spirited
b. stainless
c. stylish

**acquitted**

_____

a. obtained
b. cleared
c. realized

**squatter**

_____

a. settler
b. disorder
c. squeaker

**regretted**

_____

a. copied
b. retrieved
c. repented

---

# LESSON 5

Take your final test. Write your words in the spaces provided at the back of this book. Ask God to help you with your test.

79

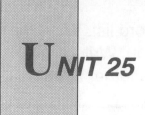

# UNIT 25

## SUFFIX RULE THREE

| | |
|---|---|
| pitiful | greediness |
| readily | melodious |
| heartiest | steadiness |
| luxurious | daintiness |
| worthily | tardiness |
| tidiness | ceremonies |
| victorious | modifying |
| copied | copyist |
| fanciful | babyish |
| glorious | accompanying |

### LESSON 1

Study these list words, using the study plan on page 7.

### LESSON 2    VOCABULARY / DICTIONARY

Use these list words in sentences. Consult a dictionary, if necessary, to understand their meanings. You may use any tense (past, present, or future) of verbs, either singular or plural form of nouns, and comparative (-er) or superlative (-est) forms of adjectives and adverbs, if you are careful to spell these alternative forms correctly.

**greediness** _____

_____

**tardiness** _____

_____

**pitiful** _____

_____

**fanciful** _____

_____

**glorious** _____

_____

**babyish** _____

_____

**steadiness** _____

_____

# LESSON 3

Write each of your list words three times on a separate sheet of paper.

## FINER THINGS

---

### SUFFIX RULE THREE

A 'y' coming after a consonant is changed to 'i' before adding a suffix unless the suffix begins with 'i.'

---

**1** Add the suffixes shown to these words.

| | -er | -est | -ly | -ness |
|---|---|---|---|---|
| **hearty** | _____ | _____ | _____ | _____ |
| **steady** | _____ | _____ | _____ | _____ |
| **ready** | _____ | _____ | _____ | _____ |
| **dainty** | _____ | _____ | _____ | _____ |
| **worthy** | _____ | _____ | _____ | _____ |
| **tidy** | _____ | _____ | _____ | _____ |
| **greedy** | _____ | _____ | _____ | _____ |

**Write:** modifying _____

copyist _____

babyish _____

accompanying _____

**Why is 'y' NOT changed to 'i' in the 4 words written at the left?** _____

**2** Write a list word that belongs with each group.

| lateness earliness timeliness | triumphant losses defeated | loveliness gracefulness clumsiness |
|---|---|---|
| _____ | _____ | _____ |

| neatness cleanliness messiness | childish immature silly | splendid grand exalted |
|---|---|---|
| _____ | _____ | _____ |

81

## LESSON 4

Take your first practice test on all words in your Unit 25 word list. Write the words on a separate sheet of paper as they are read to you. Write any words you misspelled on your practice test five times on another sheet.

## WHAT'S IN A WORD?

Write list words by adding the suffix '-ness' to the following root words:

**greedy** _____

**tidy** _____

**tardy** _____

**steady** _____

**dainty** _____

Write list words by adding the suffix '-ly' to the following root words:

**ready** _____

**worthy** _____

Write list words by adding the suffix '-ous' to the following root words:

**melody** _____

**luxury** _____

**ceremony** _____

**glory** _____

Write list words by adding the suffix '-ful' to the following root words:

**fancy** _____

**pity** _____

Add these suffixes to these root words:

**hearty+est** _____

**victory+es** _____

**copy+ed** _____

---

Write these list words. Circle the best synonym.

**modifying**

_____

a. tracing
b. changing
c. fashioning

**accompanying**

_____

a. going along
b. finishing
c. fulfilling

**copyist**

_____

a. coordinator
b. duplicator
c. transmitter

**ceremonious**

_____

a. formal
b. distinguished
c. harmonious

---

## LESSON 5

Take your final test. Write your words in the spaces provided at the back of this book. Begin and end your test with prayer.

# U NIT 26

## AU, AW, OU, OW

### LESSON 1

Study these list words, using the study plan on page 7.

| | |
|---|---|
| gaudy | flounder |
| auburn | espouse |
| auction | arouse |
| pauper | devour |
| caucus | carouse |
| awning | cower |
| lawsuit | dowry |
| brawler | drowsy |
| tawdry | prowler |
| drawback | powdery |

### LESSON 2 — VOCABULARY / DICTIONARY

Use these list words in sentences. Consult a dictionary, if necessary, to understand their meanings. You may use any tense (past, present, or future) of verbs, either singular or plural form of nouns, and comparative (-er) or superlative (-est) forms of adjectives and adverbs, if you are careful to spell these alternative forms correctly.

**drowsy** _____

_____

**devour** _____

_____

**gaudy** _____

_____

**lawsuit** _____

_____

**drawback** _____

_____

**caucus** _____

_____

**flounder** _____

_____

# LESSON 3

Write each of your list words three times on a separate sheet of paper.

## FINER THINGS

Use list words (plus a few others) to solve this crossword puzzle.

**ACROSS**

1. Sleepy
2. Very poor person
6. Showy, flashy, tawdry
9. Meeting of members of a political group or party
11. "Greet one another with an holy _____" (2 Cor. 13:12).
12. Dusty, sandy, pulverized
14. Word used to indicate choices
15. On, by, near to
18. To make merry in a rowdy, drunken way
19. Fighter, rioter
20. To struggle or wallow
21. Showy, flashy, gaudy

**DOWN**

1. Hindrance, disadvantage
3. Excite, wake up
4. A sneak, burglar
5. Advocate, support
7. Sale by bidding
8. A claim or case in court
10. To cringe in fear
13. Money or property given by a bride to her husband at marriage
15. A roof-like shade over a window
16. A reddish-brown color
17. To eat up or destroy
18. Initials for "**C** hrist- **C** entered **E** ducation"

84

Take your first practice test on all words in your Unit 26 word list. Write the words on a separate sheet of paper as they are read to you. Write any words you misspelled on your practice test five times on another sheet.

## WHAT'S IN A WORD?

Write your list words in alphabetical order.

Group the list words having these diphthongs.

**au**

**aw**

**ou**

**ow**

## LESSON 5

Take your final test. Write your words in the spaces provided at the back of this book. Begin and end your test with prayer.

# U NIT 27

# SUFFIX RULE ONE EXCEPTIONS

| | |
|---|---|
| changeable | hoeing |
| chargeable | shoeing |
| manageable | toeing |
| marriageable | agreeing |
| noticeable | agreeable |
| peaceable | fleeing |
| serviceable | freeing |
| traceable | dyeing |
| advantageous | singeing |
| courageous | tingeing |

## LESSON 1

Study these list words, using the study plan on page 7.

## LESSON 2      VOCABULARY / DICTIONARY

Use these list words in sentences. Consult a dictionary, if necessary, to understand their meanings. You may use any tense (past, present, or future) of verbs, either singular or plural form of nouns, and comparative (-er) or superlative (-est) forms of adjectives and adverbs, if you are careful to spell these alternative forms correctly.

**agreeable** _____

_____

**changeable** _____

_____

**noticeable** _____

_____

**toeing** _____

_____

**fleeing** _____

_____

**courageous** _____

_____

**manageable** _____

_____

# LESSON 3

## FOUNDATIONS

Write each of your list words three times on a separate sheet of paper.

## FINER THINGS

---

### SUFFIX RULE ONE

Final 'e' is dropped from a root word before adding a suffix beginning with a vowel.

#### EXCEPTIONS AND VARIATIONS

**1** Words ending in 'ce' or 'ge' retain the final 'e' before '-able' and 'ous' to keep the 'c' or 'g' soft.

**2** Words ending in 'oe' or 'ee' retain the final 'e' unless the suffix begins with 'e.'

**3** Some words retain the final 'e' to preserve their identity and avoid confusion with similar words.

---

**1** Combine these root words and suffixes.

| | | | |
|---|---|---|---|
| notice + able | _____ | advantage + ous | _____ |
| manage + able | _____ | courage + ous | _____ |
| service + able | _____ | hoe + ing | _____ |
| marriage + able | _____ | toe + ing | _____ |
| change + able | _____ | shoe + ing | _____ |
| trace + able | _____ | agree + ing | _____ |
| charge + able | _____ | flee + ing | _____ |
| peace + able | _____ | free + ing | _____ |

**2** Write: **notable** (note + able) _____
Does this spelling follow Rule One or an exception? ___Rule ___Exception

Write: **noticeable** (notice + able) _____
Does this spelling follow Rule One or an exception? ___Rule ___Exception

**3** Compare and contrast the spelling and meaning of these words.

| die/dye | Add '-ing' to all six of these words. Check a dictionary, if necessary. Use the preferred spelling in each case. | _____ | _____ |
|---|---|---|---|
| sing/singe | | _____ | _____ |
| ting/tinge | | _____ | _____ |

87

## LESSON 4

Take your first practice test on all words in your Unit 27 word list. Write the words on a separate sheet of paper as they are read to you. Write any words you misspelled on your practice test five times on another sheet.

## WHAT'S IN A WORD?

Write list words whose root words have these endings.

**ge**

_____
_____
_____
_____
_____
_____

**ce**

_____
_____
_____

**ee**

_____
_____
_____

**oe**

_____
_____

**ye**

_____

Write your list words in alphabetical order.

_____
_____
_____
_____
_____
_____
_____
_____
_____
_____
_____
_____
_____
_____
_____
_____
_____
_____
_____
_____

## LESSON 5

 **TESTING... TESTING...**

Take your final test. Write your words in the spaces provided at the back of this book. Begin and end your test with prayer.

88

# UNIT 28

## SUFFIX RULE 2 & 3 EXCEPTIONS

| | |
|---|---|
| reference | gases |
| preference | enemy'ɜ |
| conference | country's |
| deference | staid |
| inference | laid |
| preferable | daily |
| transferable | dryness |
| excellence | piteous |
| crystallize | plenteous |
| cancellation | beauteous |

### *LESSON 1*

Study these list words, using the study plan on page 7.

### *LESSON 2*     **VOCABULARY / DICTIONARY**

Use these list words in sentences. Consult a dictionary, if necessary, to understand their meanings. You may use any tense (past, present, or future) of verbs, either singular or plural form of nouns, and comparative (-er) or superlative (-est) forms of adjectives and adverbs, if you are careful to spell these alternative forms correctly.

**preference** _____

_____

**excellence** _____

_____

**plenteous** _____

_____

**gases** _____

_____

**country's** _____

_____

**conference** _____

_____

**daily** _____

_____

# LESSON 3

**FOUNDATIONS** Write each of your list words three times on a separate sheet of paper.

**FINER THINGS** Study the information below and look for examples among your list words.

### SUFFIX RULE TWO

In one-syllable words and in words accented on the last syllable, a final consonant after a single vowel is doubled before a suffix beginning with a vowel is added.

### EXCEPTIONS AND VARIATIONS

**1** The final consonant is NOT doubled when the accent in the root word is thrown to the first syllable after the suffix is added.

**2** The final consonant may be doubled, in adding the suffix, when the accent in the root word was ALREADY on the first syllable.

**3** In some one-syllable words, the final consonant after a single vowel is NOT doubled, purely as an exception to the rule.

### SUFFIX RULE THREE

A 'y' coming after a consonant is changed to 'i' before adding a suffix unless the suffix begins with 'i.'

### EXCEPTIONS AND VARIATIONS

**1** a). In a few words, a 'y' coming after a VOWEL is changed to 'i' before adding the suffix. b). In a few others, a 'y' after a consonant is NOT changed to 'i,' purely as an exception to the rule.

**2** In some words, a 'y' coming after a consonant is changed to 'e' before adding the suffix.

**3** A 'y' following a consonant is NOT changed to 'i' when adding { 's } to the root word.

**4** In some words having a final 'y' after a vowel, the spelling of both the root word and the suffix is altered, resulting in a wholly new spelling.

## LESSON 4

Take your first practice test on all words in your Unit 28 word list. Write the words on a separate sheet of paper as they are read to you. Write any words you misspelled on your practice test five times on another sheet.

## WHAT'S IN A WORD?

Write your list words in alphabetical order.

### EXCEPTION TO AN EXCEPTION

Notice that the following example is an exception to Exception 1 of Rule Two as expressed in Lesson 3 on page 90. Write these three words:

**ex cel' > ex' cel lent > ex' cel lence**

_____    _____    _____

Refer to the rules and exceptions outlined in Lesson 3 when completing the assignments below.

Write list words that are examples of
Exception 1 to Rule Two.
_____
_____    _____
_____    _____
_____

Write list words that are examples
of Exception 2 to Rule Two. { _____
_____

Write a list word that is an example
of Exception 3 to Rule Two. _____

Write a list word that is an example
of Exception 1-a to Rule Three. _____

Write a list word that is an example
of Exception 1-b to Rule Three. _____

Write list words that are examples
of Exception 2 to Rule Three. { _____
_____
_____

Write list words that are examples
of Exception 3 to Rule Three. { _____
_____

Write list words that are examples
of Exception 4 to Rule Three. { _____
_____

## LESSON 5

Take your final test. Write your words in the spaces provided at the back of this book. Begin and end your test with prayer.

# U NIT 29

# PER- OR PUR- / DE- OR DI-

| | |
|---|---|
| perjure | descend |
| persist | describe |
| perspire | despair |
| persuade | despite |
| perverse | despond |
| purchase | dispatch |
| purport | dissect |
| purpose | diverge |
| pursuit | dispense |
| purloin | digestion |

## LESSON 1

Study these list words, using the study plan on page 7.

## LESSON 2    VOCABULARY / DICTIONARY

Use these list words in sentences. Consult a dictionary, if necessary, to understand their meanings. You may use any tense (past, present, or future) of verbs, either singular or plural form of nouns, and comparative (-er) or superlative (-est) forms of adjectives and adverbs, if you are careful to spell these alternative forms correctly.

**persuade** _____

_____

**describe** _____

_____

**digestion** _____

_____

**perverse** _____

_____

**purloin** _____

_____

**perjure** _____

_____

**diverge** _____

_____

# LESSON 3

## FOUNDATIONS
Write each of your list words three times on a separate sheet of paper.

## FINER THINGS

**1** SPELLING AND PRONUNCIATION: Write all of your list words. Write '1' in the box if the word is pronounced with an accent on the first syllable. Write '2' in the box if the accent is on the second syllable.

☐ _____    ☐ _____

☐ _____    ☐ _____

☐ _____    ☐ _____

☐ _____    ☐ _____

☐ _____    ☐ _____

☐ _____    ☐ _____

☐ _____    ☐ _____

☐ _____    ☐ _____

☐ _____    ☐ _____

☐ _____    ☐ _____

**2** Write in the boxes the list words in these phrases. In your own words, tell what the phrases mean.

*to perjure one's self*      ☐_____  _____

*to persist in evil doing*   ☐_____  _____

*paths that diverge*         ☐_____  _____

*to purloin an umbrella*     ☐_____  _____

93

# LESSON 4

Take your first practice test on all words in your Unit 29 word list. Write the words on a separate sheet of paper as they are read to you. Write any words you misspelled on your practice test five times on another sheet.

## WHAT'S IN A WORD?

Write all of your list words, grouping them according to their beginnings.

**de**

_____

_____

_____

_____

_____

**di**

_____

_____

_____

_____

_____

**per**

_____

_____

_____

_____

_____

**pur**

_____

_____

_____

_____

_____

**Write your list words in alphabetical order.**

_____
_____
_____
_____
_____
_____
_____
_____
_____
_____
_____
_____
_____
_____
_____
_____
_____
_____
_____
_____
_____
_____
_____
_____

**Write these Bible verses on a separate sheet of paper. Use the King James Version. Circle the list words you find in them.**

I John 3:8          I Thessalonians 4:16          Philippians 2:14-15
2 Corinthians 4:8   Galatians 1:10

# LESSON 5

Take your final test. Write your words in the spaces provided at the back of this book. Begin and end your test with prayer.

94

# U NIT 30

# ENGLISH PREFIXES

| | |
|---|---|
| aground | outweigh |
| ablaze | overshadow |
| bedevil | overreach |
| beside | tonight |
| forbidden | unskilled |
| foresight | unexpected |
| misapply | undermine |
| encircle | underrate |
| embitter | withstand |
| embattled | withhold |

## LESSON 1

Study these list words, using the study plan on page 7.

## LESSON 2 — VOCABULARY / DICTIONARY

Use these list words in sentences. Consult a dictionary, if necessary, to understand their meanings. You may use any tense (past, present, or future) of verbs, either singular or plural form of nouns, and comparative (-er) or superlative (-est) forms of adjectives and adverbs, if you are careful to spell these alternative forms correctly.

**foresight** _____

_____

**encircle** _____

_____

**ablaze** _____

_____

**forbidden** _____

_____

**tonight** _____

_____

**unexpected** _____

_____

**undermine** _____

_____

# LESSON 3

Write each of your list words three times on a separate sheet of paper.

**FINER THINGS**

**1** All of the Unit 30 list words have prefixes which come from Old English or Middle English, the ancestors of our modern English. Learn these prefixes and their meanings.

| | | | |
|---|---|---|---|
| a- | = at, in, on | out- | = beyond, more |
| be- | = to make, by | over- | = above |
| en- | = in, on, to make | to- | = the, this |
| em- | = in, on, to make | un- | = not, opposite |
| for- | = not, from | under- | = beneath |
| fore- | = before | with- | = against, from |
| mis- | = wrong, wrongly | | |

**2** Study the chart above and write list words that fit these clues.

in battle _____

to apply wrongly _____

in flame _____

to make bitter _____

in a circle _____

weigh more _____

by the side _____

on the ground _____

to make like a devil _____

ordered (bid) not to _____

to reach above _____

this night _____

seeing before _____

stand against _____

hold from _____

rate beneath _____

not skilled _____

cut (mine) beneath _____

not expected _____

cast a shadow above _____

96

## LESSON 4

Take your first practice test on all words in your Unit 30 word list. Write the words on a separate sheet of paper as they are read to you. Write any words you misspelled on your practice test five times on another sheet.

### WHAT'S IN A WORD?

Write list words having these prefixes.

a- _____

_____

be- _____

_____

for- _____

fore- _____

mis- _____

en- _____

em- _____

_____

out- _____

over- _____

_____

to- _____

un- _____

_____

under- _____

_____

with- _____

_____

Write the ROOT WORDS in your list words in alphabetical order.

_____
_____
_____
_____
_____
_____
_____
_____
_____
_____
_____
_____
_____
_____
_____
_____
_____
_____
_____
_____

**Think of some other (non-list) words that have these prefixes.**

**fore-** _____

**under-** _____

**un-** _____

**mis-** _____

## LESSON 5

**TESTING...**
**TESTING...**

Take your final test. Write your words in the spaces provided at the back of this book. Begin and end your test with prayer.

# U<small>NIT</small> 31

## LATIN PREFIXES

| | |
|---|---|
| abnormal | circumnavigate |
| ascend | contradict |
| accustom | counterbalance |
| affix | demerit |
| apportion | disapprove |
| antedate | eccentric |
| bipartisan | extraordinary |
| condolence | irreverent |
| coexist | illegal |
| correspond | intermission |

### LESSON 1

Study these list words, using the study plan on page 7.

### LESSON 2

**VOCABULARY / DICTIONARY**

Use these list words in sentences. Consult a dictionary, if necessary, to understand their meanings. You may use any tense (past, present, or future) of verbs, either singular or plural form of nouns, and comparative (-er) or superlative (-est) forms of adjectives and adverbs, if you are careful to spell these alternative forms correctly.

**abnormal** _____

_____

**coexist** _____

_____

**illegal** _____

_____

**disapprove** _____

_____

**ascend** _____

_____

**irreverent** _____

_____

**correspond** _____

_____

# LESSON 3

## FOUNDATIONS
Write each of your list words three times on a separate sheet of paper.

## FINER THINGS

**1** All of the Unit 31 list words have prefixes which come from Latin, the language of the ancient Romans. This language has greatly influenced our English language. Learn these prefixes and their meanings.

| | | | |
|---|---|---|---|
| ab-, abs- | = from | con-, cor-, co- col-, com- | = with |
| a-, ac-, af-, ar- ap-, ag-, as- al-, at-, an- | = to | de- | = down, from |
| | | dis-, di-, dif- | = not, opposite, apart |
| ante- | = before | ec-, ex-, e-, ef- | = out of, from |
| bi-, bis- | = two, twice | extra- | = beyond |
| circum-, circu- | = around | ir-, il-, im-, in- | = in, on; not |
| contra-, counter- | = against | inter- | = between |

**2** Study the chart above and write list words that fit these clues. Determine the meaning of the list word by combining the meanings of the Latin-based prefix and Latin source (root) word. [KEY for below: L. = Latin].

ab + 'norma'
(L.= rule) _____

a + 'scendere'
(L.= to climb) _____

ac + custom
(habit, rule) _____

af + 'figere'
(L.= to fix or fasten) _____

ap + 'portio'
(L.= a division, a part) _____

ante + date
(L.= 'data': given) _____

bi + 'pars'
(L.= part, party) _____

con + 'dolere'
(L.= to grieve) _____

co + 'existere'
(L.= to come into being) _____

cor + 'respondere'
(L.= to answer) _____

circum + 'navigare'
(L.= to sail) _____

conta + 'dicere'
(L.= to speak) _____

counter + 'bilanx'
(L.= balance scales) _____

de + 'merere'
(L.= to earn, deserve) _____

dis + 'approbare'
(L.= to approve) _____

ec + 'centrum'
(L. = center point) _____

extra + 'ordinarius'
(L.= normal order) _____

ir + 'reverens'
(L.= reverent) _____

il + 'legalis'
(L.= relating to law) _____

inter + 'missio'
(L. = one's task) _____

99

# LESSON 4

Take your first practice test on all words in your Unit 31 word list. Write the words on a separate sheet of paper as they are read to you. Write any words you misspelled on your practice test five times on another sheet.

## WHAT'S IN A WORD?

Add root forms to these prefixes to spell list words.

ab _____          circum _____

a _____           contra _____

ac _____          counter _____

af _____          de _____

ap _____          dis _____

ante _____        ec _____

bi _____          extra _____

con _____         ir _____

co _____          il _____

cor _____         inter _____

Write your list words in alphabetical order.

_____
_____
_____
_____
_____
_____
_____
_____
_____
_____
_____
_____
_____
_____
_____
_____
_____
_____
_____
_____
_____

The prefixes ir-, il-, im- and in- mean 'in' or 'on' when used in verbs and some nouns. They mean 'not' when used in adjectives and some nouns. What do the words below mean?

| | | | | |
|---|---|---|---|---|
| *input* | *imperfect* | *illiterate* | *improper* | *invisible* |
| *insincere* | *irreligious* | *import* | *irregular* | *illuminate* |

# LESSON 5

Take your final test. Write your words in the spaces provided at the back of this book. Begin and end your test with prayer.

100

# U*NIT 32*

# LATIN PREFIXES

| | |
|---|---|
| nonessential | subjugate |
| objected | succumb |
| pervade | supernatural |
| postmortem | surpass |
| premature | suppress |
| projected | suspension |
| rejected | traverse |
| retrospect | transport |
| selection | ultramodern |
| semicircle | vice-president |

## *LESSON 1*

Study these list words, using the
study plan on page 7.

## *LESSON 2*   VOCABULARY / DICTIONARY

Use these list words in sentences. Consult a dictionary, if necessary, to understand their meanings. You may
use any tense (past, present, or future) of verbs, either singular or plural form of nouns, and comparative (-er)
or superlative (-est) forms of adjectives and adverbs, if you are careful to spell these alternative forms correctly.

**transport** _____

_____

**surpass** _____

_____

**rejected** _____

_____

**supernatural** _____

_____

**selection** _____

_____

**premature** _____

_____

**vice-president** _____

_____

# LESSON 3

## FOUNDATIONS
Write each of your list words three times on a separate sheet of paper.

## FINER THINGS

**1** All of the Unit 32 list words have prefixes which come from Latin, as did the words in the last unit. Learn these new prefixes and their meanings.

| | | | |
|---|---|---|---|
| non- | = not | se- | = aside |
| ob-, oc-<br>of-, op- } | = { in front, against<br>in the way | semi- | = half |
| | | sub-, suc-, suf-<br>sug-, sup-, sus- } | = under |
| per- | = through, thoroughly | | |
| pre- | = before | super-; (Fr.) sur- | = above, over |
| pro- | = for, forth | tra-, trans- | = beyond, over |
| re- | = back or again | ultra- | = beyond |
| retro- | = backward | vice- | = instead of |

**2** Study the chart above and write list words that fit these clues. Determine the meaning of the list word by combining the meanings of the Latin-based prefix and Latin source (root) word. [KEY: L.= Latin; Fr.= French].

**non + 'essentia'**
(L.= essense) _____

**ob + 'jacere'**
(L.= to throw) _____

**per + 'vadere'**
(L.= to go) _____

**post + 'mortem'**
(L.= death) _____

**pre + 'maturus'**
(L.= ripe) _____

**pro + 'jacere'**
(L.= to throw) _____

**re + 'jacere'**
(L.= to throw) _____

**retro + 'specere'**
(L.= to look at, to see) _____

**se + 'legere'**
(L.= to gather, select) _____

**semi + 'circulus'**
(L.= circle) _____

**sub + 'jugum'**
(L.= a yoke) _____

**suc + 'cumbere'**
(L.= to lie down) _____

**super + 'natura'**
(L.= nature) _____

**sur (Fr.) + 'passare'**
(L.= to step) _____

**sup + 'pressus'**
(L.= pressed) _____

**sus + 'pendere'**
(L. = cause to hang) _____

**tra + 'vertere'**
(L.= to turn) _____

**trans + 'portare'**
(L.= to carry) _____

**ultra + 'modernus'**
(L.= present manner) _____

**vice + 'praesidens'**
(L. = president, ruler) _____

102

# LESSON 4

Take your first practice test on all words in your Unit 32 word list. Write the words on a separate sheet of paper as they are read to you. Write any words you misspelled on your practice test five times on another sheet.

## WHAT'S IN A WORD?

Add root forms to these prefixes to spell list words.

| | | Write your list words in alphabetical order. |
|---|---|---|
| non_____ | sub_____ | _____ |
| ob_____ | suc_____ | _____ |
| per_____ | super_____ | _____ |
| post_____ | sur_____ | _____ |
| pre_____ | sup_____ | _____ |
| pro_____ | sus_____ | _____ |
| re_____ | tra_____ | _____ |
| retro_____ | trans_____ | _____ |
| se_____ | ultra_____ | _____ |
| semi_____ | vice-_____ | _____ |

### WORD NOTES

The English word 'postmortem,' meaning 'after death,' is taken directly and without change from two Latin words: 'post' = *after* and 'mortem' = *death*.

The meaning of the list word 'vice-president' can be traced from Latin. 'Vice' means 'instead of.' President comes from 'praesidens,' which, in turn, comes from Latin for 'pre' (before, in front of) and 'sedere' (to sit). Thus, a president literally is one who 'presides' or 'sits in front.' A vice-president is someone who presides or rules 'instead of' or 'in the place of' a president.

# LESSON 5

Take your final test. Write your words in the spaces provided at the back of this book. Begin and end your test with prayer.

# UNIT 33

# GREEK PREFIXES

| | |
|---|---|
| atheist | epidemic |
| anarchy | hypercritical |
| amphitheater | hypocrite |
| analysis | metaphysics |
| antarctic | megalopolis |
| apostle | antithesis |
| cataract | synthesis |
| catastrophe | sympathy |
| diameter | antipathy |
| emphasis | apathy |

## LESSON 1

Study these list words, using the study plan on page 7.

## LESSON 2          VOCABULARY / DICTIONARY

Use these list words in sentences. Consult a dictionary, if necessary, to understand their meanings. You may use any tense (past, present, or future) of verbs, either singular or plural form of nouns, and comparative (-er) or superlative (-est) forms of adjectives and adverbs, if you are careful to spell these alternative forms correctly.

**hypocrite** _____

_____

**atheist** _____

_____

**apostle** _____

_____

**epidemic** _____

_____

**sympathy** _____

_____

**diameter** _____

_____

**catastrophe** _____

_____

# LESSON 3

Write each of your list words three times on a separate sheet of paper.

**FINER THINGS**

**1** All of the Unit 33 list words have prefixes which come from Greek, an ancient language before Latin. The New Testament part of the Bible was originally written in Greek. Learn the prefixes below and their meanings.

| | | | |
|---|---|---|---|
| a-, an- | = not, without | em-, en- | = in, on |
| amphi- | = both, around | epi-, ep- | = upon |
| ana- | = up, back, through | hyper- | = over |
| anti-, ant- | = against, opposite | hypo- | = under |
| apo-, ap- | = from | meta-, met- | = beyond, change |
| cata-, cat- | = down | mega-, megalo- | = large, great, strong |
| dia- | = through | syn-, sy-, syl-, sym- | = with, together |

**2** The root words in your list words also come from Greek. Study the prefixes above and Greek words below. Write list words to fit the clues below.

theos = God
lysis = the act of loosening
pathos = feeling
stellein (root of 'stle' in 'apostle' = to send)
metron = measure
demos = people
thesis = a placing
polis = city
archos = ruler
strephein (root of 'strophe' in 'catastrophe') = to turn
arktos = bear, Ursa Major, north
arassein (root in 'kataraktes,' [sheer, abrupt] and the 'ract' in 'cataract') = to smash or strike
kritikos = able to discern or judge
hypokrites = actor on a stage
physikos = natural
phainein (root of 'phasis' in 'emphasis') = to show, indicate

| | |
|---|---|
| one who believes in no God | a disease "on many people" |
| without ruler or rule of law | overly "judgmental" or critical |
| theater "in the round" | one who "acts" insincerely |
| a "loosening up" for study | beyond what is natural |
| a terrible "down-turn" | a very large city |
| an "abrupt downfall" of water | something "placed" against |
| opposite of the north (arctic) | something "placed" together |
| one who is "sent forth" | feelings "shared together" |
| a "through-measure" | without feelings |
| forcefulness of "indication" | feeling opposite or against |

105

# LESSON 4

## TAKING STOCK

Take your first practice test on all words in your Unit 33 word list. Write the words on a separate sheet of paper as they are read to you. Write any words you misspelled on your practice test five times on another sheet.

## WHAT'S IN A WORD?

### GREEK ALPHABET

| | | |
|---|---|---|
| Αα | Alpha | a |
| Ββ | Beta | b |
| Γγ | Gamma | g |
| Δδ | Delta | d |
| Εε | Epsilon | e |
| Ζζ | Zeta | z |
| Ηη | Eta | ē |
| Θθ | Theta | th |
| Ιι | Iota | i |
| Κκ | Kappa | k |
| Λλ | Lambda | l |
| Μμ | Mu | m |
| Νν | Nu | n |
| Ξξ | Xi | x |
| Οο | Omicron | o |
| Ππ | Pi | p |
| Ρρ | Rho | r |
| Σσ | Sigma | s |
| Ττ | Tau | t |
| Υυ | Upsilon | u,y |
| Φφ | Phi | ph |
| Χχ | Chi | ch |
| Ψψ | Psi | ps |
| Ωω | Omega | ō |

Add root forms to these prefixes to spell list words.

a_____          epi_____

a_____          hyper_____

an_____          hypo_____

ana_____          meta_____

cata_____          mega_____

cata_____          anti_____

ant_____          anti_____

apo_____          amphi_____

dia_____          sym_____

em_____          syn_____

The English word 'alphabet' is derived from the names of the first two letters of the Greek alphabet: 'alpha' and 'beta.' See the Greek alphabet at the right. Notice that the last word of the Greek alphabet is 'omega.' In Revelation 22:13, Jesus says: "I am Alpha and Omega, the beginning and the end, the first and the last." By this He means that all things have their origin and destiny in Him and that He is the source and determiner of all things. St. Paul, in speaking to some Greek philosophers about Jesus, quoted one of their own poets: For in Him we live, and move, and have our being... (Acts 17:28).

# LESSON 5

## TESTING... TESTING...

Take your final test. Write your words in the spaces provided at the back of this book. Begin and end your test with prayer.

# UNIT 34

## DISCRIMINATING SYNONYMS

| discover | courage |
| invent | bravery |
| capacity | gallantry |
| ability | fortitude |
| genius | heroism |
| talent | cheerfulness |
| axiom | merriment |
| maxim | comfort |
| proverb | consolation |
| adage | solace |

### LESSON 1

Study these list words, using the study plan on page 7.

### LESSON 2 — VOCABULARY / DICTIONARY

Use these list words in sentences. Consult a dictionary, if necessary, to understand their meanings. You may use any tense (past, present, or future) of verbs, either singular or plural form of nouns, and comparative (-er) or superlative (-est) forms of adjectives and adverbs, if you are careful to spell these alternative forms correctly.

**discover** _____

_____

**ability** _____

_____

**courage** _____

_____

**merriment** _____

_____

**proverb** _____

_____

**invent** _____

_____

**comfort** _____

_____

*BE CAREFUL HOW YOU USE THESE WORDS!*

# LESSON 3

## FOUNDATIONS

Write each of your list words three times on a separate sheet of paper.

## FINER THINGS

**1** Study the following concepts. Write the list words described.

_____ We discover what existed before.

_____ We invent what did not exist before.

_____ Capacity is the power of receiving.

_____ Ability is the power to do.

_____ Genius implies extraordinary and high gifts within our nature.

_____ Talent implies natural strength of intellect or ability to execute a skill.

_____ Courage is 'firmness of spirit that meets danger without fear.'

_____ Bravery is a kind of courage which shows itself in 'outward acts.'

_____ Gallantry is 'adventurous courage.'

_____ Fortitude is 'passive courage' (strength) that bears up nobly under trial.

_____ Heroism calls up all forms of courage and devotes them to a 'noble cause.'

_____ Cheerfulness is a happiness that is a habit of the mind.

_____ Merriment is outward excitement or noisy expression of happiness.

_____ Comfort is a general state of well-being and ease.

_____ We take consolation when we are in sorrow; it is comfort in a time of grief.

_____ We take solace, a comforting refuge, in some off-setting diversion, such as prayer, books, or the company of friends and supporters.

_____ An axiom is a self-evident truth.

_____ A maxim is a guiding principle.

_____ A proverb is a common saying, expressing a significant idea or principle.

_____ An adage is a very old proverb.

## LESSON 4

Take your first practice test on all words in your Unit 34 word list. Write the words on a separate sheet of paper as they are read to you. Write any words you misspelled on your practice test five times on another sheet.

## WHAT'S IN A WORD?

| Write your list words in alphabetical order. |
| --- |

The following noun endings signify the STATE, QUALITY, OR ACT of the person, place, or thing being named by the root noun.

**ace, acy, age, al, ance, ancy, don, ence, ency, hood, ing, tion, ion, ism, ment, mony, ness, ry, ship, the, tude, ty, ity, ure, y**

*happiness = the state of being happy*    *friction = the act of rubbing*
*recital = the act of reciting*    *supremacy = the quality of being supreme*

Write list words that have any of the above endings.

_____    _____

_____    _____

_____    _____

_____    _____

_____    _____

Unscramble these list words.

**nettal** _____    **moxia** _____

**tromcof** _____    **ixmam** _____

**vennit** _____    **roscvide** _____

**shomire** _____    **sunige** _____

## LESSON 5

Take your final test. Write your words in the spaces provided at the back of this book. Begin and end your test with prayer.

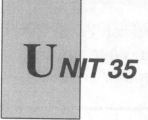

# U NIT 35

## CHANGE OF ACCENT

| | |
|---|---|
| abstract | produce |
| compound | project |
| contrast | record |
| converse | transplant |
| escort | survey |
| ferment | rehash |
| frequent | redress |
| perfume | export |
| permit | reject |
| present | discharge |

### LESSON 1

Study these list words, using the study plan on page 7.

### LESSON 2    VOCABULARY / DICTIONARY

Use these list words in sentences. Consult a dictionary, if necessary, to understand their meanings. You may use any tense (past, present, or future) of verbs, either singular or plural form of nouns, and comparative (-er) or superlative (-est) forms of adjectives and adverbs, if you are careful to spell these alternative forms correctly.

**present** _____

_____

**record** _____

_____

**reject** _____

_____

**converse** _____

_____

**permit** _____

_____

**abstract** _____

_____

**frequent** _____

_____

# LESSON 3

**FOUNDATIONS**

Write each of your list words three times on a separate sheet of paper.

**FINER THINGS**

All of the words in your Unit 35 word list may be used as verbs AND either nouns or adjectives ... or all three, in some cases.

When used as VERBS, the primary accent is always on the LAST SYLLABLE.

When used as NOUNS or ADJECTIVES, the primary accent is always on the FIRST SYLLABLE.

Find each of your list words in a dictionary or thesaurus and write a brief definition or synonym for each, first as a verb, then as a noun or adjective.

| VERBS | | NOUN/ADJECTIVE |
|---|---|---|
| _____ | abstract | _____ |
| _____ | compound | _____ |
| _____ | contrast | _____ |
| _____ | converse | _____ |
| _____ | escort | _____ |
| _____ | ferment | _____ |
| _____ | frequent | _____ |
| _____ | perfume | _____ |
| _____ | present | _____ |
| _____ | produce | _____ |
| _____ | project | _____ |
| _____ | record | _____ |
| _____ | transplant | _____ |
| _____ | survey | _____ |
| _____ | rehash | _____ |
| _____ | redress | _____ |
| _____ | export | _____ |
| _____ | reject | _____ |
| _____ | discharge | _____ |
| _____ | permit | _____ |

111

# LESSON 4

Take your first practice test on all words in your Unit 35 word list. Write the words on a separate sheet of paper as they are read to you. Write any words you misspelled on your practice test five times on another sheet.

## WHAT'S IN A WORD?

**Write your list words in alphabetical order.**

The following list words may be used as verbs, nouns and adjectives. Write the words.

abstract _____     present _____

compound _____    record _____

Write these list words. Draw a line between the syllables.

abstract _____     permit _____

compound _____    survey _____

contrast _____     rehash _____

converse _____     redress _____

escort _____      export _____

ferment _____     reject _____

frequent _____     discharge _____

perfume _____     transplant _____

The following list words have different syllable divisions, depending on whether they are used as verbs or nouns/adjectives. Write the words. Draw lines between syllables. Add primary accent marks where needed.

| *VERBS* | *NOUNS/ADJECTIVES* |
|---|---|
| present _____ | present _____ |
| produce _____ | produce _____ |
| project _____ | project _____ |
| record _____ | record _____ |

# LESSON 5

Take your final test. Write your words in the spaces provided at the back of this book. Begin and end your test with prayer.

# UNIT 36

## 'L' OR 'LL'

| | |
|---|---|
| almighty | welcome |
| millennium | welfare |
| millionaire | bellboy |
| artillery | belfry |
| military | bulrushes |
| intelligent | metallic |
| parallel | pollution |
| diligent | pollinate |
| altogether | alliance |
| already | hallelujah |

### LESSON 1

Study these list words, using the study plan on page 7.

### LESSON 2    VOCABULARY / DICTIONARY

Use these list words in sentences. Consult a dictionary, if necessary, to understand their meanings. You may use any tense (past, present, or future) of verbs, either singular or plural form of nouns, and comparative (-er) or superlative (-est) forms of adjectives and adverbs, if you are careful to spell these alternative forms correctly.

**diligent** _____

_____

**pollution** _____

_____

**already** _____

_____

**almighty** _____

_____

**intelligent** _____

_____

**bellboy** _____

_____

**welcome** _____

_____

## LESSON 3

**FOUNDATIONS**   Write each of your list words three times on a separate sheet of paper.

**FINER THINGS**   Which list words are suggested by the clues?

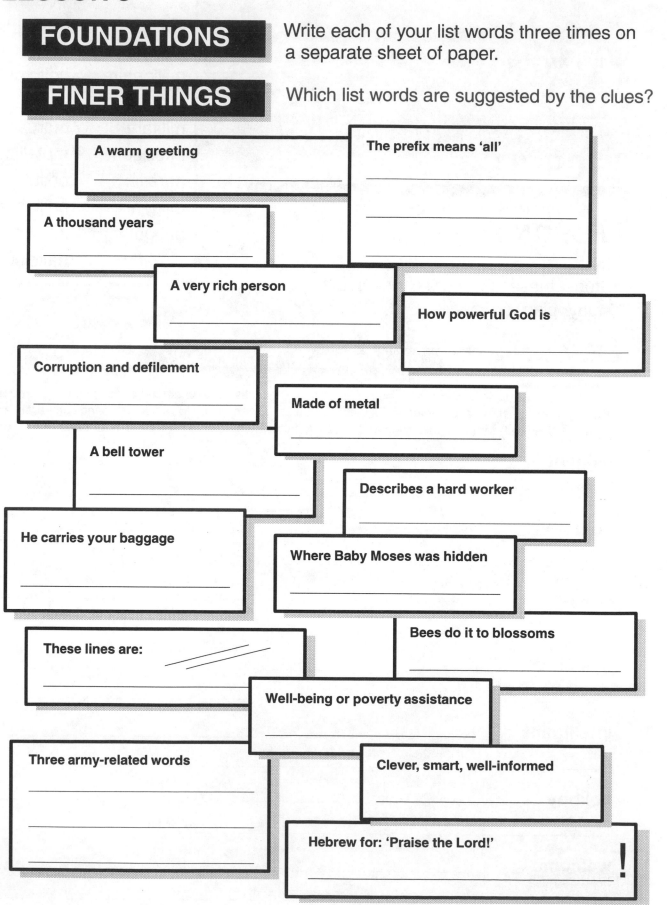

A warm greeting
_____

The prefix means 'all'
_____
_____

A thousand years
_____

A very rich person
_____

How powerful God is
_____

Corruption and defilement
_____

Made of metal
_____

A bell tower
_____

Describes a hard worker
_____

He carries your baggage
_____

Where Baby Moses was hidden
_____

These lines are: ╱╱
_____

Bees do it to blossoms
_____

Well-being or poverty assistance
_____

Three army-related words
_____
_____

Clever, smart, well-informed
_____

Hebrew for: 'Praise the Lord!'
_____ !

114

## LESSON 4

Take your first practice test on all words in your Unit 36 word list. Write the words on a separate sheet of paper as they are read to you. Write any words you misspelled on your practice test five times on another sheet.

## WHAT'S IN A WORD?

Write all list words that have double 'L'.

_____

_____

_____

_____

_____

_____

_____

_____

_____

Write all list words that have at least one 'L' standing alone.

_____

_____

_____

_____

_____

_____

_____

_____

_____

Write your list words in alphabetical order.

_____

_____

_____

_____

_____

_____

_____

_____

_____

_____

_____

_____

_____

_____

_____

_____

_____

_____

_____

The ancient Hebrews have given the world a word which is known among Christians of nearly every nation, tribe and tongue. It is:

### Hallelujah!

This word is formed from two Hebrew words: 'hallelu' and 'Jah.' The first means 'praise' and the second is a short form of one of the names of God, a name we write as Yahweh or Jehovah. This word is often translated as THE LORD. Psalms 146 & 148-150 all begin and end with this word. Read these psalms and memorize some of your favorite verses.

## LESSON 5

Take your final test. Write your words in the spaces provided at the back of this book. Begin and end your test with prayer.

## UNIT 1 TEST

_____

_____

_____

_____

_____

_____

_____

_____

_____

_____

_____

_____

_____

_____

_____

_____

## UNIT 2 TEST

_____

_____

_____

_____

_____

_____

_____

_____

_____

_____

_____

_____

_____

_____

_____

## UNIT 3 TEST

_____

_____

_____

_____

_____

_____

_____

_____

_____

_____

_____

_____

_____

_____

_____

## UNIT 4 TEST

## UNIT 5 TEST

## UNIT 6 TEST

## UNIT 7 TEST

## UNIT 8 TEST

## UNIT 9 TEST

| UNIT 13 TEST | UNIT 14 TEST | UNIT 15 TEST |
| --- | --- | --- |
| _____ | _____ | _____ |
| _____ | _____ | _____ |
| _____ | _____ | _____ |
| _____ | _____ | _____ |
| _____ | _____ | _____ |
| _____ | _____ | _____ |
| _____ | _____ | _____ |
| _____ | _____ | _____ |
| _____ | _____ | _____ |
| _____ | _____ | _____ |
| _____ | _____ | _____ |
| _____ | _____ | _____ |
| _____ | _____ | _____ |
| _____ | _____ | _____ |
| _____ | _____ | _____ |
| _____ | _____ | _____ |
| _____ | _____ | _____ |
| _____ | _____ | _____ |

**UNIT 16 TEST**

**UNIT 17 TEST**

**UNIT 18 TEST**

| UNIT 19 TEST | UNIT 20 TEST | UNIT 21 TEST |
| --- | --- | --- |
| | | |
| | | |
| | | |
| | | |
| | | |
| | | |
| | | |
| | | |
| | | |
| | | |
| | | |
| | | |
| | | |
| | | |
| | | |
| | | |
| | | |
| | | |
| | | |

**UNIT 22 TEST**

_____

_____

_____

_____

_____

_____

_____

_____

_____

_____

_____

_____

_____

_____

_____

_____

**UNIT 23 TEST**

_____

_____

_____

_____

_____

_____

_____

_____

_____

_____

_____

_____

_____

_____

_____

_____

**UNIT 24 TEST**

_____

_____

_____

_____

_____

_____

_____

_____

_____

_____

_____

_____

_____

_____

_____

_____

## UNIT 25 TEST

## UNIT 26 TEST

## UNIT 27 TEST

**UNIT 28 TEST**

**UNIT 29 TEST**

**UNIT 30 TEST**

## UNIT 34 TEST

_____

_____

_____

_____

_____

_____

_____

_____

_____

_____

_____

_____

_____

_____

_____

_____

_____

## UNIT 35 TEST

_____

_____

_____

_____

_____

_____

_____

_____

_____

_____

_____

_____

_____

_____

_____

_____

_____

## UNIT 36 TEST

_____

_____

_____

_____

_____

_____

_____

_____

_____

_____

_____

_____

_____

_____

_____

_____

_____